ANGER IN THE CLASSROOM

ANGER IN THE CLASSROOM

FINDING FREEDOM FROM ANGER

A **HANDBOOK** FOR **TEACHER** AND **LEARNER**

GLENN NYSTRUP, M.S.

Epigraph Books
Rhinebeck, New york

Anger in the Classroom: Finding Freedom from Anger: A Handbook for Teacher and Learner © 2019 by Glenn Nystrup

All rights reserved. No part of this book may be used or reproduced in any manner without written permission from the author except in critical articles or reviews. Contact the publisher for information.

Paperback ISBN 978-1-948796-61-3
eBook ISBN 978-1-948796-62-0

Library of Congress Control Number 2019937584

Cover design by Amara Projansky, Colin Rolfe, and David Perry
Book design by Colin Rolfe

Epigraph Books
22 East Market Street, Suite 304
Rhinebeck, NY 12572
(845) 876-4861
epigraphPS.com

ACKNOWLEDGMENTS

In the scale of things, there has been invaluable support and inspiration at points along the way in the life of *Anger in the Classroom*. In gratitude...

Do	Jeremiah Horrigan—for starting it off with a strong do
Re	David Remer—for the first rounds of editing and for putting readings into practice (Where the rubber hits the road)
Mi	Maya Projansky—for the right note at the right moment—bridging the first half-step
Fa	For the rich music of family (Bros)—with special note for grandsons Asher and Ezra: endless inspiration and joy, (and for our mischievous play) beautiful chord and discord
Sol	For all of the students and teachers who have allowed me to be learner and teacher, and have given so much to one another
La	Key notes along the way (Jonathan Wolfman, Margot Slade, Jason Stern, Dory Mayo, Amara Projansky)
Ti	For teachers found, after schooling was past—Frank Crocitto and Jerry Toporovsky -to bridge the next half-step
Do	To you the reader—may the life in this book connect with the life in you!

TABLE OF
CONTENTS

INTRODUCTION XI
| *How to Use this Book* XIII

CHAPTER ONE: **ANGER IN THE CLASSROOM** 1
| *The Face of Anger* 1
| *You Are an Angry Person* 4
| *Manifestations of Anger* 5
| *Anger Themes* 9
| *Education Themes* 10
| *Teacher Anger* 13
| *End-of-Chapter Questions* 16

CHAPTER TWO: **PERSPECTIVE AND ANGER** 18
| *About* 18
| *Self-Perspective* 22
| *Changing Perspective* 24
| *Bias and Expectation* 29
| *Ask* 33
| *The Two-way Arrow* 35
| *End-of-Chapter Questions* 38

CHAPTER THREE: **SAFETY** 39
   Safe Environment 39
   How to Fall 42
   Keeping Record 46
   End-of-Chapter Questions 60

CHAPTER FOUR: **ANGER TOOLS** 61
   Teacher as a Classroom Tool 61
   Observation 65
   Perspective 70
   Techniques 71
   Language—and Play 78
   Anger as a Useful Tool 95
   Class-wide Anger Topics 104
   End-of-Chapter Questions. 106

CHAPTER FIVE: **CLASSROOM SETTING AND ANGER** . . 108
   Human Desire to Learn 108
   Trust 110
   Chaos Level 111
   When to Step In 115
   Stimulating Classroom 118
   Discipline Without the "Dis" 121
   "Classroom Dance" 123
   End-of-Chapter Questions 124

CHAPTER SIX: **CLASSIFIED** 126
   Special Education and Anger—and Fair vs. Equal 126
   Giving Students an "Out" 130
   ASD 135
   EBD 146
   ADHD 154
   Other 162
   End-of-Chapter Questions 163

TABLE OF CONTENTS

CHAPTER SEVEN: THE INNER APPROACH 164
- *What is meant by "Inner Approach"?* 164
- *Pre-occupied* 166
- *Inner Practices* 167
- *Transformation* 176
- *End-of-Chapter Questions* 179

CHAPTER EIGHT: THE TEACHER I.E.P. 181

CHAPTER NINE: THE FUTURE 190
- *The Long Role of the Teacher* 190
- *Our Finest Gift* 192
- *Freedom From Anger* 194
- *The Process in Review* 201
- *End-of-Chapter Questions* 204

APPENDIX: ENDNOTES 205

INTRODUCTION

Throughout infancy, childhood, and youth there are experiences that will propel a being along a path of growth and expansion, and experiences that will retard or reverse such growth. These experiences might be internal or external to the person, intentional or accidental, and in line or not with one's needs at that precise moment in time.

We, as teachers and as parents, will have a major influence in the shaping of these experiences, although in no way do many experiences in childhood need to be choreographed or constructed. Far from it, there are certain spontaneous conditions and actions that will contribute to the fullness of being and rightness of place for the young.

Anger occupies a position of danger. The harm generated through internal or external anger could be significant. Not always is anger a danger, but the potential for this demands attention from anyone who is frequently in contact with the young, or whose charge it is to help these persons grow. To ignore it is to be at peril.

In the pages to follow we will explore aspects of anger and our relationship with it—that which arises within us and that which comes at us. We will look at ways in which this strong emotion might be used as a tool for growth or as an indicator of areas worthy of our focus. We will look at specific techniques, as well as explore *perspective* and the ability to influence *it*. There is much to learn at every stage of teaching.

Although anger is not alone in its ability to inhibit or stimulate growth in a person, it is a valuable subject to explore. We can learn from anger and we can be damaged by anger as well. For this reason alone it is important to address. Yet another aspect of anger makes it valuable to study. It is ubiquitous and familiar to every human being. It is easy to access in our lives and even appears to be growing in presence on a grander scale.

A teacher is not immune from the touch of anger, and this could play a substantial role in the smooth-function or dysfunction of a classroom. It is important for teachers to clearly realize this and to address both the forceful and subtle influence of anger in every classroom. While managing student anger is widely viewed and written about, far less attention is given to a teacher's seeking to understand the presence of anger in himself and in the classroom around him.

If the case-stories and exercises in this book inspire the reader to engage, explore, and/or expand, then I hope it is done without end, for the vibrancy of this undertaking is a gift that each of us might appreciate for a life-time.

These pages have been written through the eyes of a beginning teacher, novice teacher, and teacher of forty-five years—as well as a child, student, and parent. All of these are part of me. All of these contribute to the perspectives and insights that have enriched the life of this author, and continue to do so. While there is much toil, demand, and frustration in the life of a teacher, there is also the potential for considerable joy—that which has brought so many into the field of teaching, of working with the young. May we not forget this, and may it buoy us.

INTRODUCTION

HOW TO USE THIS BOOK:

As a teacher I know that there is often an optimum time to introduce new material to a student or to review prior material. Although it can be difficult to accommodate varied ability levels in a large classroom, nevertheless, the principle still holds. One result of material being presented too early is that the student will gain little more than a vague intellectual idea of what is presented, without any depth or real understanding. The student is simply not yet ready to grasp or appreciate the basics of the material, let alone its nuance. By itself this is not the problem. The sad part is that when the same or similar material is presented at a later time, when the student is mature enough to make the needed connections and find joy in the learning, the opportunity will be lost. I see this happen often. The student will look and think (consciously or not), "Oh. I already know this" or "I don't like this," and the material will not penetrate. It will not be available. A deep understanding and appreciation can be forever out of reach, an important link lost.

This can be true, as well, in the reading of a book filled with material rich in potential self-exploration and spring-points for personal learning. A book itself does not have all of the answers. It cannot. The reader's interaction with book content, and what she is able to make use of in her own effort, is where the true strength resides. The weakness of a book lies in the difficulty in putting it down and choosing to make that personal exploration, rather than simply moving on to read further interesting material. The difficulty, if an interest is piqued, is in *not* turning to the next page.

Numerous case-stories and exercises will be presented in this book as a *call to action* - to help the reader/participant gain learning and appreciation from the content, and not move on with little more gained than mild curiosity satisfied.

EXERCISE 1:
Accept/Reject

> As readers, I ask that you consider this maxim: "Neither Accept nor Reject—Test for Yourself." When you see something or hear something, hold it without judgment long enough to see how it resonates with you. Give it space, before it's dropped internally into a category of this or that, of yea or nay. Whatever it is, take it as a starting point. I find that only by allowing an objective stance within myself—no matter what the activity or stimulus is, no matter what my immediate reaction is—am I able to step into areas of understanding where I haven't gone before, or be able to see or hear things from a new perspective: a liberating feeling and a clearer view.

One approach to using this book is to read or skim through the entire book, to get the "lay of the land," and to determine where it would be best for *you* to begin. Select a section and work with it for a while—a week or a month could yield results. This might then make the choice of the next section obvious to you. Work with all sections that might be of value. Then, in a year (perhaps even precisely one year), revisit the same sections of the book and the effort made. See if you are the same or if you've changed. Revive the effort. Either way there will be more to gain.

Another approach is to work with a partner. This can be done informally, giving mutual support, or in a way in which two people are closely linked in their effort, comparing notes on similar exercises at chosen intervals. Whatever your choice, honesty—with yourself, your efforts, and your level of success—is important in order to be effective.

The aim of this book is to empower each teacher, within any school system, with sufficient skill, vision, and flexible perspective so that she can take appropriate action in any setting she finds herself in. The goal is to create a vibrant learning environment where neither anger, nor even the teacher, is the force in charge. Rather, it is that deliciously rich state of passionate learning.

CHAPTER ONE

ANGER AND EDUCATION

> "The most harmful force known to humanity is not high-tech weaponry but raw anger. Anger is lightning in a bottle, and the bottle is us."
> —**Alan Reder**

THE FACE OF ANGER:

Ralph has been a teacher for four years, and it's not what he expected. His class is large, his time feels compressed, leaving little time for connection to his students. He had pictured meaningful conversations, noble guidance, and inspiring breakthroughs with students. There have been some, but few. So few. Instead, squeezed into a monotonous role he seemingly cannot break out of, he feels exhausted at the end of each day. He feels he is mired down in a mountain of paperwork, watered-down teaching, and a sense of impotence—leading to frustration, disappointment, and an overall anger. Appreciation is sinking. Anger is rising.

James is a dedicated math teacher. His middle school students are not all lovers of math, or even tolerant of it. This might not be a problem except that James, as a boy and a man, hasn't developed much understanding or versatility regarding his own emotional landscape. He has a shallow well of experience upon which to call for empathy or personal examples to help guide his students. He doesn't have the patience to follow long-term strategies to help them. He doesn't know how to engage with their lack of connection with the class material. He is beset by anger at small, increasingly frequent complaints about math and the goading actions of the students. Now the disconnect appears to be building into a contest for the boys in class. If they cannot succeed in the academic contest, perhaps they can succeed in another—pushing the teacher to the breaking point. Success here equates to a student's elevated standing in the eyes of his peers, and a lowered standing for the teacher.

Louise likes her high-school students most of the time. But when they don't show the respect she feels she deserves, anger begins to permeate her—and sometimes she can't help but express it. When asked, several of these students complained that she treated them like little children. Others said she was too harsh and threatened them too much. She did tend to jump back and forth between these two ineffective approaches, often finding it difficult to engage the students and to employ appropriate discipline or class management techniques when needed, or even simple, direct communication. Many students said that she did try to reach them at times, but they just couldn't connect with her— and without connection, many efforts fail.

Kevin is a student who has come into his GED class angry. He is quarrelsome today, and this isn't his usual state. We, his teachers, wonder at this. Before we get a chance to ask, he says, "I want to take a practice test today, the OPT." Ah! So that's it. He's anxious, fearful that he won't do well. He knows that parts of the test will be difficult for him. We give him space.

Dasha, a student, is a young adult who tells us that she wished someone had disciplined her when she was a child. She had been left on her own and didn't develop in all the ways she wished she had —too much room to get into trouble and into bad habits. This does not, however, make her any easier to manage in class, even with her keen awareness of the impact of her difficult behavior. She's usually fine in class until we ask the wrong thing of her, such as to not interrupt when someone else is speaking. She *throws a fit*. She's "touchy", even though she recognizes the weakness of it and doesn't want to be controlled by her emotions. And she's inclined to argue her position until she runs out of breath, leaving teachers in a difficult position.

Terry is a fifth grader who just failed another math test. He feels angry, thinks he's dumb, and wants to get out of school but can't. He knows that he must come back tomorrow for more—and the day after that and the day after that. If he doesn't make himself numb, his anger might explode. Whether the direction for Terry is anger or depression, leading to acting out or drawing inward, more will be demanded of the teacher.

Glenn loves to teach, though at times his anger is piqued in the classroom. His anger arises when he finds himself getting angry at students. As strange as this statement may seem, it's accurate. It indicates a twofold "whammy" for Glenn. Generally he has good skills at side-stepping anger, but when he fails at this, when he finds himself angry with a student, he gets angry with himself for his perceived failure. Now he is angry at two people. This doesn't help his emotional/mental state or the resolution of the problem.

The many faces of anger, in both teacher and student, present to each teacher a challenge to engage in myriad ways—from grand to subtle, from common to unique, from harsh to soft. The ability of each teacher to move swiftly in one selected direction or another to deal with "hotspots" in the classroom will determine the mood as well as the level of trust and communication between all classroom participants. This is not a small job. Yet, when done well, it can be a thoroughly engaging experience. Seeing students grow before our eyes is one of the most satisfying rewards for teachers to experience, and one of the primary draws to the profession.

Yet interference in the form of anger can strike at any time in the classroom. What do we do when students don't come to class prepared, or regulations around cell phone use or side-talking in class are continually ignored, or larger problems appear? Does anger begin to arise? What happens when we have disagreement with our mentor or administrator, or have conflict with a parent, or get overwhelmed with testing and paperwork busy-ness? What happens when we say, "I just can't do this anymore," but we must? We can't just ignore all of this. Not for long, anyway. We can't simply turn off feelings.

Devoid of feeling I would become a robot. I would completely lose the spark of joy and excitement that I still experience when teaching. To become a teacher who experiences no joy in teaching is to create a situation of drab, torturous monotony for all in the classroom. I wish to move in the opposite direction of this—toward fostering a vibrant classroom where energized students explore and delve and fail and succeed, where there is trust in classroom safety and fair rules and genuine support, where anger and other difficult hurdles can be faced directly with skill and caring and with a sense of potential learning.

YOU ARE AN ANGRY PERSON:

> You, Reader, are an Angry person!
> Would you agree? To what degree?
>
> "No, no, not Me!
> You just can't see—
> I'm clean and clear entirely from that weakness
> gripping Ann Marie, Tucker Lee, and Desiree—
> but I'm not them and they're not me!
> So I'll tell you once more, finally,
> before I set to cursin'—
> ***I'm not an angry person!!"***

MANIFESTATIONS OF ANGER:

Anger Manifestation Chart: A Sampling of 27/∞ (27 Out of Infinity)

	Symptom	Anger-Link	Check Box
1	I don't want to face the day picturing work	dread	
2	I keep a distance from my students	self-protective, distant	
3	I don't really trust **those** students	bias	
4	I complain about students, co-workers, administrators	complaining	
5	I've lost the bounce in my step in the classroom	feeling heavy, leaden	
6	I resent the amount of paperwork piled on me	resentful	
7	I bristle at teacher evals or any bit of criticism	reactive, bruised ego	
8	I react more strongly than suits the moment	inappropriately reactive	
9	My body holds tension and does not move smoothly	tense	
10	I give sharp retorts when I don't want to	irritable	
11	Time moves slowly (I check the clock too often)	slogging	
12	I am emotionally on edge, a fire easily sparked	impatient	

	Symptom	Anger-Link	Check Box
13	I suppress an inner rage at my boss for dumb and unfair actions	critical and volcanic	
14	I wish my co-teacher would retire	disdain, disapproval	
15	I enter the classroom with anxiety	anxious	
16	I over-discipline	harsh	
17	I under-discipline	fearful of controlling anger	
18	My thoughts are often negative	pulled toward the negative	
19	I feel betrayed or let down	blame	
20	I feel unjustly targeted	righteous indignation	
21	I want to kick something (or someone)	frustration	
22	I get angry at myself	self-judgment	
23	Anger holds on too long— it doesn't dissipate quickly	my anger is sticky	
24	I notice that I do things in a sly manner	mistrust and disconnect	
25	I imagine how to get back at others	revenge	
26	I miss what some students are saying	lost in imagination, displeased or bored with the current moment	

	Symptom	Anger-Link	Check Box
27	I say things that evoke reaction, and I'm surprised	invisible anger	

These Anger-Links represent a selection of the innumerable ways in which anger may manifest or be encouraged to grow. They might also act as subtle or obvious pointers toward deeper anger. A reader might find it difficult to identify many Anger-Links because the links hide from our self-view. Unless we are practiced at observing such characteristics, we may not have the vision for them. The reader might, however, get a *sense* of connection to some of the twenty-seven links listed above even when a clear mental link is absent. A way to begin exploring would be to check such item boxes above.

A reader might, as well, get a strong sense of, "Oh this one is definitely not me!" Yet, what often occurs is that the things we most strongly react to in this way are the ones that a quiet part of us wants to keep deeply hidden, while in actuality they do apply.

EXERCISE 2:
How Angry?

Scale: Check a box if you see the manifestation, or one like it, in yourself at least once a week, or if you suspect that the manifestation fits you. (For your eyes only—try not to deceive yourself.)

Checked Boxes - quantity:
1 to 4   Are you really alive and breathing? Saintly?
5 to 9   Human—one who deals with symptoms of anger
10 to 19   Still human—one who carries anger
20 to many   Yes, still human—an angry human?

Like all tests and all scales, it's difficult to lock a person into a set position. Many factors come into play in the world of actuality, factors that can shape the outcome dramatically, giving at times very different results. Any result of the above scale is meant to act as a guide to an interested participant in the attempted observation of held personal perspectives. It is a tool, not a judgement.

None of us are locked into the boxes we check. We can change if we wish to strongly enough, and variations may be observed from day to day (or hour to hour). One way to discover what value there might be in such an activity is to take the check-the-box challenge and to simultaneously give a strong effort to the exercise below. What can be seen from this?

EXERCISE 3:
Manifestations of Anger

Add to the list above. What traits do you display when angry in or out of the classroom? Can you notice quiet rumblings of anger in you that are not readily visible, to you at least? Dare you ask a friend what they see of anger in you?

What do you feel and how does it manifest? Observe in three different settings:

1. While at school, whenever you think of it look around, notice your feelings and behavior. Aim to do this, just for a moment, five distinct times each school day.
2. Observe your feelings and behavior during heated moments in the classroom or at school. Observe with the intention of later taking notes on this, even if you don't record the notes (though it would benefit you to do so), or at the least of recalling the experience. This will inwardly help you to more deeply accept the importance of a serious approach.
3. When you have a quiet moment, in or out of school,

review your school day related to the specific observations we are discussing here. Can you see yourself act, can you picture yourself? Imagine how an observer might describe you.

Stay with this for two weeks. Then let it go and try another exercise. Come back to it after a break. You may, however, notice that your sensitivity will have increased in this arena and observations will be more forthcoming without intentional effort needed. If the exercise has seemed useful then try adding a bit of increased intention to all interactions relating to emotionally charged moments.

ANGER THEMES:

- Anger in the classroom is often not understood—to disastrous effect for both student and teacher.
- Communication between teachers and students often lacks the depth necessary to adequately address highly-charged situations.
- Children are seldom given instruction in how to clearly and openly deal with emotions such as anger, and they struggle with the feelings, the expression, the receiving, and the manifestations of anger.
- These children turn into adults who continue to struggle with many aspects of anger.
- Abandon into anger can take one on a wild and precarious ride.
- To be in anger means to be in separation—from others, from our own best interest, from a possible objective perspective, from a solution to a problem.
- To be in separation can lead to agitation and increased anger.
- It *is* possible to understand anger—to learn about and to learn from anger.

- It *is* possible to prepare for many potentially volatile classroom situations.
- Anger, with certain efforts, can provide a useful opportunity for the classroom and for the individual—promoting growth and personal strength.
- Many teachers want the passion of *teaching*, of seeing and experiencing growth and connection with their students - but feel worn down by a system that allows little time for this, and makes many other demands.
- Many students want the passion of *learning* -but feel worn down by a system that allows little time for explorative or creative learning. Many do not associate school with this passion or vibrant growth in any way - though there might have been hope of this at some point.

EDUCATION THEMES:

Goal—To identify aspects of education which relate directly to a teacher's ability to prevent, manage, and avoid contributing to anger in the classroom.

EDUCATION PRESCRIPTION

Teaching is not an exact science. There is much room for interpretation, personal perspectives, adaptation, trial and error (called *learning*), and different paths toward favored outcomes. Exploration and questioning are natural ways to improve our teaching abilities. These writings are not intended solely to hand out prescription but to open up opportunities and new arenas for teacher and student, touching the considerable possibilities that each of us hold. Anger and emotionally charged moments may be addressed by many of these possible approaches, both classic and novel.

ADAPTABILITY

Our ability to change the way we act and relate during stressful moments can be strong or weak in us depending on what we have learned and how we apply this to each situation:
- strong if a teacher moves with purpose from one position to another or to morph some aspect of an interaction,
- strong when a teacher can hold steady in the face of chaos or uncertainty while watching for an appropriate direction in which to move,
- weak when the teacher chooses to (figuratively) close his eyes and run away, without a reasonable go-to position,
- weak if the action is to follow someone or something when it is not known why (including at times when this comes from within us).

DISCRIMINATION

Often there are subtle distinctions or delineations between things (settings, thoughts, observations, emotions, ideas…) that remain below the level of our attention—easy to miss. As we learn to bring them forward, to see that which we could not before see, we open vast new possibilities. This then offers us an increased degree of discrimination. Clarity of vision and action become more available to the teacher.

E.G. — TRENDING

Consider this simple, though not so subtle, example of two similar yet different trends in education—the programs: *Teaching Tolerance* and *Appreciating Diversity*. Both are intended to support the positive interaction of students from differing backgrounds, beliefs, practices, etc. *Teaching Tolerance* has done much to raise awareness and create harmony for a wide range of students - so has the drive at *Appreciating Diversity*. Yet when we look at the words *tolerance* and *appreciation* we experience a notably different quality. To *appreciate* difference can be far richer than to merely *tolerate* difference. Yet there are times and places where one approach might be far more applicable than the other. Or one might precede the other. To be clearly aware of this will be a valuable tool for the teacher.

INNER LANDSCAPE

Many personal attributes are difficult to see in ourselves. Material in each of the chapter sections below is designed to help the reader see herself more clearly as a person and as a teacher, and thus be in a position to feed or starve that which is seen. In this way a teacher has a strong hand in her own self-development.

What is seen in a person's words and actions is often a manifestation of what is occurring inwardly. When contemporary culture and its schools minimally address the inner life of students, there is much of our inner landscape that remains shadowy and out of focus for each of us—*and worthy of exploration.*

JOY

Throughout the effort that we make as teachers to improve and to deliver the best service to our students and families, there is much appreciation and joy to be found. May we not forget!

GUIDANCE

For each child there will be an extensive experience of education, formal or not. Years of education will accrue over time and constitute a wealth of experience, for good or ill. As teachers we will be an integral part of this long path. Imagine being able to know just what to do—to step into the student's school experience, to push here, lift there, step aside at this moment, or offer wisdom at another moment—in order to inspire each student, or to help her rise to her finest potential at that time. Our actions could be gross or subtle, open or secret, depending on the need. The results, the growth, for the student could seem almost magical as great strides are made; (although I believe that this could become a new norm). But this will not take place, even with the best of intentions, if there is not practical and deliberate effort made on the part of the teacher to grow and to discover more about himself as a teacher and as a person.

The teacher is the key to all of this. The teacher is the model. The teacher is the guide. When a teacher is able to learn about himself and develop skills that support continued learning from his classroom experiences and his life experiences, he can bring vibrant, first-hand, knowledge to students. Deeper learning will become available to all, together with a significant sense of accomplishment.

TEACHER ANGER:

If one were to peruse books, blogs, sites, and periodicals she could find nearly limitless information and opinions on how to address anger that arises in students of varying ages and situations, as well as a surprisingly small quantity of information related to the anger existing and erupting (or simmering) in teachers throughout these classrooms. This is a problem, since the teacher is the focal point in the classroom—the setter of tone, the conductor of the orchestra. If managing one's own anger is an ultimate goal for each student, so that the teacher or some other outsider doesn't need to do the managing, then the teacher must be agile in addressing her own anger as it arises. Only in this way can she avoid potential damage through the expression (or harboring) of anger, be a valuable role model in the classroom, and truly understand and empathize with the experience of the student. With this knowledge she will be in a position to directly communicate that understanding to each student and help him to gain similar skills and insight.

I've seen anger in the classroom through decades of schooling and of teaching. At times anger has seemed appropriate to the setting and even quite useful, but mostly, it's just been ugly. It has caused pain and disruption, torn at hearts and self-confidence, and taken events far from a vibrant learning environment. Sometimes it's simply the explosive, negative energy bomb that spreads a dark cloud wide over everything. Sometimes it's an arrow fashioned of words and emotions shot at someone. Whether by design or through an unguarded moment while under the spell of anger, it is a weapon that can kill enthusiasm and possibility, leaving lasting scars—scars that can forever affect the learning setting and relationship between student and teacher.

It has become clear to me that in order to help students and myself grapple with the many ways that anger can affect us, a specific effort is needed. And that effort must start at home, in me the teacher. If I respond to a difficult situation without clarity, without a picture of where I wish to proceed or what tools to use, I'll have haphazard results. Clearly, I don't wish to invite more hazards in this direction.

E.G. — WHAT GOAL?

This is a story about Darnel. Darnel sat at a table with the task of categorizing objects according to multi-criteria. It had taken guidance and then practice for him to be able to complete this task on his own, but he did it. When Darnel completed the task the assistant said, "Well done," disassembled it and asked him to repeat the exercise. Darnel complied.

His instructor at the time, the assistant, had received target goals from the special-educator (who was not currently present). *The goal*: when Darnel was able to perform the task ten times independently his effort would be considered a success, his competence established.

When Darnel's assembly was again taken apart and the assembly cycle was repeated a third time he started to become agitated. Finally, he threw the materials across the room in frustration and anger. The assistant ran down the list of behavioral management techniques in her mind in order to control his actions. Her anger increased as she now became frustrated and reacted to his reaction, heightening the tension in the room. When later reporting on the session she stated that Darnel was not successful. He failed to complete the task of repeating the exercise, and he had problems with anger control.

What she did not understand was what the actual goal was. It was to manage a complex set of tasks of categorizing and sorting. At this he succeeded. The goal was not to be able to display the capacity to repeat a complex exercise ten straight times, watching his creations destroyed between each effort, then doing it all over again. When he became angry and frustrated at the adult for this destruction, it was the adult who was failing—failing at recognizing that the instructions provided by the special-educator were either inappropriate or inappropriately applied. Darnel acted as most any person would—with frustration. He may indeed benefit from help with how to express frustration, but that is a different issue. (Efficient review of this entire incident would look closely at the position and instruction of the special educator who set up the activity—how the assistant was informed of the activity, how instructions were worded, and what the supervision or oversight was like? These questions and more would be asked.)

FOCUS LOCUS—THE PROBLEM IS OUTSIDE

One basic theme of this book is connected to a common human habit—the habit to look outward to find a solution to a problem, rather than inward. This can range from trying to change a friend or family member in order to improve a relationship, to changing where I live in order to create a new life for myself. This holds true in the classroom, as well. When tempers and strong emotions flare, the tendency is to focus primarily on managing a student's behavior rather than to look to my own position, as teacher, in this situation. Managing immediate anger is, of course, important—yet a weak approach if the effort ends there.

Perhaps in a particular setting I'm not directly involved in the heated interaction. The events seem to be far away from me. Yet, at the least, my handling of the situation and my nurturing of communication and trust beforehand will go a long way toward relieving stress and mending emotional wounds. The exploration of my own feisty emotions, and inviting students to explore theirs, can help me know at any moment what an effective course of action might be. It could be, too, that I am directly contributing to difficult classroom moments or moods—through a word, a look, a tone, a bias.

So, as I look to ensure a safe classroom for all during a heated classroom moment, I learn to look simultaneously to myself for understanding. I look for knowledge about volcanic moments arising in the classroom or the smoldering anger that erodes self-confidence, communication ability, civil interaction with others, and personal well-being. Many learning experiences, varied and rich, may arise from these efforts—for both student and teacher.

END-OF-CHAPTER QUESTIONS:

Regarding the story of Darnel—

1. Does the challenge placed before the student actually reflect the target goal? What is the target goal, and how appropriate does it appear to be?
2. Is there inherent failure built into the activity? If so, how?
3. What is the role of an assistant teacher when given a task? Is it okay to question, and/or assess the task that has been handed down? To adjust it?
4. Could the teacher (any level teacher) benefit from better understanding her own anger? How might it be worth the effort?

5. How can teacher emotions play a role in the fairness of reporting when assessing student behavior? Do you have your own personal observations of this?

Other Questions—

6. What themes have you noticed regarding anger in schools or the nature of anger in general?
7. What stories can you recall regarding teacher anger? Are there insights to be had from these?

CHAPTER TWO

PERSPECTIVE

"Civilization began the first time an angry person cast a word instead of a rock."
—**Sigmund Freud**

ABOUT:

Perspective is a most personal thing. Our very character is defined by how we view what is around us and within us. It determines how we interpret information and experience, how we relate to others, and affects our mood and *state*. For a teacher working in a classroom, or for anyone working with children, the ramifications of our perspectives are of great importance. They will help shape our relationships with students and set our outlook on each day. Whether perspective is immediate and related to the setting, or of a more deeply held nature locked within a set belief system—the effects guide and shape our actions and interactions.

Conversely, the exploration and study of perspective, both in general terms and when specific to the individual, can be quite fruitful and liberating. Much can be learned about oneself, about the possibilities inherent in knowledge about perspective, and how to apply this understanding in the classroom and elsewhere. Let's explore.

Definition—Oxford English Dictionary (OED):
perspective. True understanding of the relative importance of things; a sense of proportion. (1)

Definition—Merriam-Webster Dictionary (MW):
perspective. The faculty of seeing all the relevant data in a meaningful relationship; the proper or accurate point of view or the ability to see it; objectivity. (2)

One might get a sense of the significance of perspective, reading the definitions above. Words like "meaningful," "accurate," and "importance" suggest value. Further reading indicates that these values can have useful applications and can help provide links in our understanding that broaden our knowledge.

Or—perspective can be seen simply (from another perspective) as *any particular view-point*, as presented in the MW definition: *A mental view or prospect.*

One thing that is not presented in any of the above definitions is the source of our "seeing," except for the word "mental." Do we, however, see with our mental capacity alone, or might "seeing" include our senses and emotions, for example? Can sensing and feeling inform how and what we see, as well as how we interpret all of it?

A limited perspective, by definition, is often associated with a lack of understanding or appreciation of perspectives held by individuals around us. This can easily lead to anger and conflict as individuals and ideals cross paths, in school or out—especially when tolerance of differences decreases. Conversely, a broadening of one's perspective to include views dissimilar to our own can expand our understanding and appreciation of all that is around us. Links to new knowledge, in myriad forms, open up and become available to us. We expand.

This simple formula is the force behind many school programs and policies, such as "Appreciating Diversity", reading varied authors, inviting guest speakers, and going on field trips. It's all about expanding the perspective of students—intellectually, emotionally, and experientially—as they grow into adults. Along with core knowledge and skills, the delivery of novel experiences for students is an ingredient of essential programming that will insure that the desire and ability of each student to learn and grow will remain intact and, in fact, increase. Also, while understanding and appreciation of the ways of others increases, negative reactions to them decrease—an important ingredient in diminishing anger in any classroom or school.

Study abroad programs are further examples of providing opportunity for expanded perspective for students.

E.G. — STUDENTS

"I learned so much about what I wanted to do while I was abroad. The confidence I gained studying abroad was incredible. I can go anywhere now."
—**Kelly Case, State University of New York at New Paltz (SUNY/New Paltz). (3)**

"The value of the research went further than the research we conducted as a team. I also had the opportunity to observe the families, eating habits, languages, and medical systems of a culture vastly different from my own, I learned how careful observation was necessary to gain a better understanding of why and how Diabetes was highly prevalent in this malnourished society."
—**Jayden Kiernan, SUNY/New Paltz. (4)**

For teachers, learning through the expansion of perspective might come in the form of workshops, in-service trainings, and mentor programs. In addition, access to the greater potential that each teacher holds can be made through the personal efforts of each individual - one of the primary focal points of this book.

EXERCISE 4:
Important to You

List three topics related to teaching that are important to you, which you can more deeply explore: Let's select one example: student inquisitiveness—or more measurably: student willingness to ask questions.

Following this example, observe students in your classroom and ask yourself these and similar questions:
- Are there particular times when students asking questions seems to be more forthcoming than at other times?
- What is the setting/topic/tone at those moments?
- What is your part in this? Does your action/mood/patience/expectation affect student willingness to ask questions?
- What can you observe that appears to squelch or encourage a student impulse to ask questions (peers, teacher, setting, emotional withdrawal, deep curiosity...)?
- Can you identify students who have changed considerably over time in their willingness to ask questions?

Encouragement or discouragement with student questioning may be noticed in teachers around us, as well. These can be very useful observations as we relate this to our own experience and behaviors.

Record observations on the questions you have written for yourself.

Use this procedure with each of the three topics you chose to focus on.

We continue to follow the *perspective* thread: *Spect-* the root of *perspective* indicating to *watch* or *see*.

Relate this to the role of a teacher. It is the goal of a teacher to develop a view of herself *as* a teacher, with:

Intro*spect*ion—observation of the effects of her attitudes and actions on others

Self-in*spect*ion—to be aware of inner drives, motivations, cherished beliefs

Per*spect*ive—to be aware of how she *sees* others

Shifting per*spect*ives—to be able to see from the point of view of others

Re*spect* for students—to truly see students - to "see again" and beyond the outer shell or manifestation

Con*spect*ion—to increase "observation with understanding"

SELF-PERSPECTIVE:

It can be difficult at times to reconcile the picture we might have of ourselves as a teacher entering the field of education with high hopes and aspirations, with a later picture of a stretched-thin, sometimes frustrated, angry teacher. When complaining about the overload of paperwork or standardized testing, or the impatience and agitation we might feel toward students or administration, the view of oneself as a valuable, supportive teacher can seem distant. It's too easy to belittle ourselves and to note how we don't stack up to the heroic teachers we have seen in films like *Stand and Deliver* with Edward James Olmos, *Blackboard Jungle* with Glenn Ford, *Mona Lisa Smile* with Julia Roberts, or *The Great Debaters* with Denzel Washington. Movies capture but pieces of a teacher's life, both in and out of the classroom, according to what the director wishes. I do believe that each of us could be made to look quite heroic, as well, if the right director took on the project.

There is always someone better at any particular attribute or any skill that I have. So what! We are human creatures encompassing both the strengths and foibles that go along with this opportunity to be alive.

PERSPECTIVE

We are parents, friends, sons, daughters, wives, husbands, adversaries, confidants, and more. We experience events that lift us, and others that depress us. This is a given. We experience pain, frustration, joy, and satisfaction at a job well done. What can we do to move closer to the ideal that we can so easily see, and that we wish to be, and might feel so far away from?

The first step is to realize that change is possible. No matter where we currently stand, we can move toward growth. We can take stock of where we are, how we function, the patterns that we fall within, and use this information to our benefit. There are specific ways that this can be done, and effort that must be applied. Any change that occurs that is not brought forth by intent will be accidental or, literally, unintentional. This change may or may not be of use. It might even be detrimental to our aim. It's easy to see the value of establishing aim—be it short-term objectives or long-term goals. Without aim we don't know where to set our sails or steer our rudder.

Case-stories, exercises, and text will be presented within these pages to help create the settings and conditions conducive to the type of growth we speak about. It is our option to work to the level we wish, depending on how much we want to accomplish and how much we are able to invest. Each of us holds the possibility of growth, of improving in any direction we wish. Though wish alone is not enough, a strong *wish* can supply tremendous energy for our efforts.

The next step is to strengthen and employ tools that are available to us, such as the skill of *observation*, and to realize the importance of this for teachers. (See *Anger Tools*, Chapter Four.) Julia and David Gorlewski, in referring to several aspects of teachers as *critical observers* state: "Threaded throughout...is the importance of exploring who we are in terms of our experiences and our identities so that we can articulate the perceptual context we bring to observable events." (5) This is not the last time we will note the close relationship between observation and perspective, with perspective influencing observation, and observation as a means of liberating perspective. From here, engaging the tools available to us, we can learn and we can also develop new tools—again, expansion.

CHANGING PERSPECTIVE:

E.G. — CHARLES AND RANDY: CHANGING PERSPECTIVE IN INDIVIDUALS

I worked with a co-teacher named Randy who was having difficulty getting the classroom to quiet and attend to the lesson at hand or, in fact, any of the current lessons he was delivering. One boy in particular, Charles, had a loud behavior and often brought other students along where his personality led them. Randy felt unable to change the situation and asked me to step in. He was upset with Charles, our loud student, and anger was clearly building. I also was a teacher of these students for different subjects, and chose to take direct action at this moment. I asked Charles to join me in a different room where we could speak alone. I spoke with a seriousness meant to remind him that I had options in regards to his behavior. "Charles, I don't know if you've noticed, but your behavior often has a big influence in the classroom. I believe that you can use this strength to move in a number of different directions. Will you lead the other students, by being a role-model, to a place where you'll all be able to learn? By giving the teachers a chance to do their job everyone can benefit. Then both the teachers and the students will feel respected."

I knew that he cared, but was getting caught up in the enjoyment of laughing and raising a ruckus. I had to judge whether this tactic might work and if he would be open to a change in perspective. He thought my suggestion as a good idea, welcomed the responsibility, and acted with maturity. Things immediately improved in the classroom. This all took about ten minutes. I approached with respect, both for him as a person and for his ability to understand and to appreciate the current classroom situation at a deeper level than was previously being engaged in. Randy asked me about the change he had witnessed, and a fruitful discussion followed.

Several changes in perspective (active or potential) can be noted in this three-way interaction. Such as:
- Glenn's view of Charles (Was my view of Charles correct? My request could have backfired.)
- Randy's view of the situation (How could it be approached differently next time?)
- Randy's view of Charles (an asset versus a liability)
- Charles' view of his role (from trouble-maker to class leader supporting learning & classroom effort)
- Charles' view of his own character and strengths (extrapolating the strengths in this situation to other settings)
- Charles' view of Glenn, who expressed a faith in Charles' ability to be a leader in the class and to make a cooperative effort to encourage a vibrant learning setting (working in a sense as peers—allowing Charles to step to a higher level of responsibility)

E.G. — TWO-ROOM SCHOOLHOUSE: CHANGING PERSPECTIVE IN A CLASSROOM OF STUDENTS

As director/teacher at a small private school, one day I found myself facilitating a discussion with the students of the school involving *seeing with new eyes*. Once a week we had a community meal where one student was responsible for bringing in a main course dish, one brought a salad, and another brought bread. On this particular day I left early for a meeting at another school. Speaking with teachers later, I was told that it all went well, except that several small items were left on the floor at the end of the event, which students did not clean up.

The next day we spoke about the meal and many aspects of it. I opened the interaction to the students and was met with *a wall of silence,* so I acted as catalyst. As we began to talk about the little bit of trash left on the floor, not a big deal, I thought of several ways it could be approached. I thought of the oft-used line, "Your mother doesn't work here." I thought of a discussion about how disrespectful it is to the people who allow us to have our school here. These approaches would be classics. I thought also of a discussion about how easy it is for us to be careless with our actions and to ignore the repercussions of these actions, a discussion which could move things a bit closer to the possibility of direct student insight. But today we went in a different direction.

After a period of discussion, students began to see where the conversation was headed due to questions I asked. We had made the effort to have a special day together. Certain students planned, prepared, and brought in food. All students helped set up tables and set the tables. Food was served. Food was eaten. Conversation was shared as well. Everyone then helped clear the tables, put the tables and chairs away, and clean the room. And it was at this point that the process fell apart. It was not a major difficulty by any means. Yet – it was significant.

"Every day", I explained, "every moment, we are either learning something new or reinforcing what we already know, what we already do. This is simply in the nature of being human. What happened here was a very fine process that proceeded well until it neared the end. It was not completed. It didn't come *full circle*. Full circle would mean that there would be no sign at all that an event had taken place—a clean end ready for a clean start. So, by this action, what were you teaching yourselves?" I asked, "—to not complete what you began—to leave it unfinished? This might not seem to be a significant thing. It was only a bit of debris left on the floor. But there'll come a time when you do wish to fully finish what you've begun, and you will have weakened yourselves by these actions, by this *practice*. The results of our actions accumulate—both in our bodies and our minds."

PERSPECTIVE

I could have furthered the discussion by looking at how common it is for any process to break down toward the end, as attention weakens. I have even seen death occur (not at a school) as a result of this late-process relaxation of carefulness. But I let it go for now. The students were silent at this point, each sitting with her/his thoughts. My hope was that this would be a specific, as well as a more sweeping, lesson about observing oneself—even or especially in the seemingly insignificant moments—and striving for the best.

E.G. — SUDDEN SHIFT: CHANGING PERSPECTIVE IN MYSELF (UNEXPECTEDLY)

One day, as I was eating a snack in middle school, I had a sharp mental shift in perspective. I had eaten half of the Twinkie I held in my hand and suddenly found myself staring at the remaining half. It did not look like something familiar to me. I continued to stare at this cream-filled confection while the words formed in my mind: "This is not food." The shock of it stunned me. I was standing there holding something that looked alien—and never had it occurred to me before that such a mainstream snack, eaten by millions, could be something unlike food. It was simply a compilation of texture and taste. We were always told by smiling faces in magazines and elsewhere to enjoy this fine treat. My perspective on all foods changed in that instant, never to return to the naiveté that had existed before.

E.G. — TRASH CAN TARGET: CHANGING PERSPECTIVE IN MYSELF (WITH OUTSIDE HELP)

I was reading a children's book to my grandsons, Asher (age ten) and Ezra (age eight). I had only a vague recollection of reading this book many years earlier. I had a growing sense as I read, however, of the negative nature of nearly every character in the book. But it had won a national book award—said so on the cover—and I was caught up in the joy of reading to two grandsons who were snuggled up beside me, so I let the vague disturbance remain just that—vague. I took no action.

I didn't listen to an inner perspective that was clearly there on some level.

The boys' father had been nearby for the reading and spoke with me afterward. "This book is negative and cynical and not even well-written. The characters have little respect for one another or even for themselves. Is this the kind of influence we want to bring into their lives?" I agreed, and was grateful for the additional (external) perspective that helped me "see" what I was not able or willing to see on my own. This book is now "off the shelf" (and in the recycling bin) in my library, where many others are ready to stand in its place. The next effort will be to be sure of the book before I begin reading. The boys were upset with me for cutting it off and in general it *is* best to continue what you start, but this was hopefully a useful lesson for them as I explained my reason for tossing the book.

A WARNING TO READERS

A great deal of negativity is buried in books and other writings in the form of humor, clever plot lines, and strong characters. Cynical, disillusioned characters do exist, both in books and in actuality, but the literary use can be way overdone, especially when there is no distinct purpose other than to get eyes on the page—a shallow goal.

E.G. — READY TO WORK: CHANGING PERSPECTIVE IN MYSELF (INTENTIONALLY)
Speaking with a friend, whose perspective I trusted, about how difficult it can be to get up for work each day, he said, "Learn to love it, to love going to work. Change your attitude." "Sure, no problem, I'll just snap my fingers," I was thinking. But I tried it. I put effort into it—and the result surprised me. I developed an entirely new appreciation of the opportunity of getting up and going to work each day. It was as though I had *willed* this to happen, and it came about. It felt like magic on one hand, and

on the other it seemed to simply be something that was within my ability when I applied a certain force.

THE USE OF WILL

Applying *will* in this way, as described above, can produce strong results. A further benefit is that our will itself has been strengthened. As a muscle gets stronger through repeated use, so does *will*. Yet with *will* dimensions can develop that go beyond what was there at the start. A muscle can turn into stronger muscle, but must always be a muscle. *Will* can actually transform the way we relate to the world. This is a jump to a level beyond the initial ability of *will*—to get things done. Here we can, to a degree, change the way we are.

BIAS AND EXPECTATION:

Bias is a reflection of the perspectives a person holds. In this way bias is often invisible to the bearer, because we are blind to many of the perspectives we inhabit. Unless individuals make an intentional effort to notice bias in themselves, the view that they get of their own bias is most often accidental. The problem with the invisibility of bias is that it can color every moment of our lives and penetrate every action we take while we have no knowledge that this is happening. It is especially important that *teachers* understand the biases they hold, for without this clarity of vision there is little chance of providing an even playing field for students in the classroom—and every teacher-student relationship will be affected in unpredictable ways.

> *"Teachers and teacher educators must become keenly aware of their own cultural heritages, identities, and biases before they can help their students..."*
> —**Daniel P. Hallahan et al.,** *Exceptional Learners* **(6)**

There are additional ways in which to consider bias in education. In *Exceptional Learners*, two forms of bias are cited below within these cautions on testing:

> *"1. Tests give only clues about what the student has learned.*
> *2. Test scores must be interpreted with recognition of the possible biases the test contains.*
> *3. Testing alone is an insufficient bias for classifying a student or planning an instructional program."* (7)

We are pressured as teachers to consider what we actually test when we give a test. Is it IQ—or cultural knowledge? Is it analyzing ability—or vocabulary? Then the questions arise, "How will this uncertainty influence testing results, how will the student feel about herself, and how will this affect behavior in school?"

Julia and David Gorlewski refer to one challenge perspective plays in standardized testing, in which students are being asked to participate with ever greater frequency, and teachers must observe ever more carefully.

"Although they (standardized tests) are designed to be inclusive, broad in scope, and universally applicable within an identified context, the final published product reflects a series of decisions made by a group (or groups) of people. ...these decision-makers may be unknown to (and separated from) those impacted by the standards... any decision privileges certain perspectives and marginalizes others, both through commission and omission." (8)

Bias can place students at an unfair advantage or disadvantage, depending not on a student's achievement levels, but on some other person's views—nothing more. Bias then can actually change the performance levels of students, as we observe in the following section on expectation.

EXPECTATION RELATED TO BIAS

Bias affects not only how each of us interprets all that we see, but also what we expect to see. This in turn will influence the behavior and performance of each of the students in our class. Whether a teacher holds expectations consciously or blindly, students will be affected and results will be *colored*. We can see here the extreme importance of teacher awareness of bias-in-self. Consider this example:

E.G. — DENNIS: SHARP OR DULL?

Dennis is speaking to his teacher in the 6th grade. He is asked the question, "If you had a choice of living in a city or in a country setting, what would you choose and why?" Dennis stands there, says nothing for a full minute, appearing to be thinking. He then gives an answer to the question. The teacher thinks, "This seems to be a slow-witted boy. I will need to pay attention to this." She might next time try to help by answering the questions for Dennis or giving strong cues, so that he won't feel uncomfortable or embarrassed. She believes that she is helping the student.

Then picture a different teacher asking the same question. Dennis gives an identical response. Yet here the teacher thinks, "This boy thinks carefully before answering the question. He must have rich inner dialogue and experience. I will give him time, and help foster this strength."

The expectations are quite different—and the short and long-term effects will differ, leading Dennis down varying paths, ones that the teacher expects. Where one teacher might encourage, the other might pass over the student or give overmuch support.

The source of teacher expectations may come from internal or external stimuli, and might be accessible or out of reach for the teacher. A goal here is to attempt an objective, open starting point with each student, in each moment—holding expectation at bay—and then to proceed with caution.

NOTES ON TEACHER EXPECTATION:

- Expectations grow out of something; some thought, idea, feeling, sight, imagining, or a combination of these, perhaps from many years past. If we can notice our expectations we can look for what drives them.
- Expectations may be conscious or unconscious on our part as teachers.
- Expectations create blinders where much new information and insight is cut-off, made unavailable. Since the peripheral vision is blocked and nothing is allowed to enter from the side where much new knowledge lies, *tunnel-vision* prevails. The person holding fast to her expectations fends off threats to held beliefs. Stasis and decline, rather than growth and learning, becomes the default position.
- When a teacher holds strong expectations he places limits on himself as well as the student, both in view and in performance.
- Each expectation pulls the teacher into some future moment, thinking ahead, categorizing, coloring, losing the richness of the moment now. There is a feeling of being off-balance.
- Bias is often unseen by the holder, and may be doubted or denied when confronted, at times with a considerable level of emotion.
- I become rigid and brittle if expectation is allowed to hold position over time.
- Expectations can dampen any enjoyment I might experience in an action or interaction - whether I simply follow the rut I have created or I have to deal with contrary occurrences that have developed.
- When a person expects to feel or experience a certain way, to have a "good" day or "bad" day, often he will. Things will tend to manifest as he expects them to. This emphasizes the importance of consciously directing or influencing his expectations, rather than allowing them to influence and direct him.
- Expectation can lead *toward* or *away* from anger.

- Teacher expectation will influence a student's success in class (academically, socially, personally).
- A student's success in school will influence his comfort, level of engagement, frustration level, and mood.
- A student may readily react to a teacher's held expectations and attitudes.
- Student frustration can quickly lead to anger and behavioral challenges.
- Positive teacher expectations can lead a student away from anxiety, frustration, and anger.

ASK

To ask is to open a door. That is, the very act of asking creates an energy that can produce specific results or open a channel to new possibilities. As teachers we can do this for ourselves or our students. We can, as well, model the process for students so that they might better understand the possibilities.

E.G. — PETER: SEEKING INFORMATION

Peter, a co-worker who had worked with me for a short time, was new to classroom teaching. Actually, his entire classroom teaching career so far was about four weeks. He had observed me in the classroom and was trying to learn as much as he could as quickly as he could. Peter asked if I had any advice or observations to give on his classroom performance. I thought for a moment then said, "Don't act friendly. Be friendly." He gratefully accepted this and went on to weave it into many moments of classroom action. He was able to extrapolate what he learned in this short exercise and apply it to a wide array of situations regarding actions, emotions, and what works best in the classroom.

It was easy to see from my perspective, a veteran teacher with many varied classroom experiences, that, although he was by no means an unfriendly person, his friendly persona in front of the class appeared subtly forced and ingenuous. This simple advice led to action on his part that did not even appear, on the outside, different than it had before, but held an entirely different feeling and quality to it. It also allowed for genuine connection to be made with the students—one of the primary qualities of emotions. His heart was now engaged along with his head, and as he later told me, "Small change. Major impact!"

E.G. — LARA: TO OPEN UP A FLOW

Lara was taking an online college class in her career field and had reached an impasse with a specific assignment. She was stuck and could not move at all on the lengthy paper she was tasked to write. She tried various things, but none of them brought help. Finally she turned to a friend to ask for help. She did this via text and waited for a return message. The message was not readily forthcoming, and Lara was left seemingly in the same situation she had been in before. Yet this was not so. As she waited for the response that did not come until much later, she found that something had opened up in her, and she began to write with ease. As she described it, "I just opened up to getting help, and that seemed to be enough. I opened, and the flow of writing opened. I didn't even need to get direct help from my friend."

To ask for support or help might seem like a small act. It can, however, contain many facets that make the asking difficult or complex. Some individuals will hesitate to ask for help from anyone (*Real men don't ask for directions!*). Others may readily ask for help, yet have difficulty truly hearing what is offered, or ask so often it loses meaning and impact. Help may be asked for with general or specific goals in mind, or from friends, professionals, or higher powers. The point here is to open up the possibility of learning from and leaning on the act of *asking*. When we ask, there occurs an opening in us—a level of vulnerability, of acknowledging "I don't know," or "I can't do this on my own." An answer could be specific knowledge, emotional strength, or recognition of direction. Something new and useful might enter if a willingness is there.

THE TWO-WAY ARROW

When I am conscious, aware of myself, at the same moment that I observe something/someone near me, the line of my attention resembles a two-way arrow—one point directed at the thing I observe, and the other toward me. This valuable human capacity enables us to maintain a penetrating perspective on ourselves as we simultaneously observe people, settings, and/or sequences around us. This allows us to notice the way we feel, think, and act at any given moment— interwoven with that which is viewed. We learn about ourselves.

As teachers we are expected to monitor ourselves in numerous ways in an ongoing manner. We observe our voice and the response of students to this voice. We observe our actions, and more subtly, our prejudices and our perspectives. We try to understand the consequences of all this. We notice how—as we learn about our classroom over a period of months—management and communication become enriched. We notice our teaching effectiveness as we become more experienced at teaching and guiding over a period of years. Insights and ever more subtle detail and nuance may result from the two-way-arrow practice, in addition to the natural maturing of an experienced teacher. Growth might then be exponential (the rate of growth itself increasing).

The aim that is indicated here is to act and to observe at the same time. We observe how we act as we interact with what we observe around us. For a teacher this is of great value. The more fully we can see and grasp a moment in the classroom, the more effectively and smoothly we will be able to take action.

Additional insight and understanding is available as we observe ourselves internally as well as externally, at any moment, in any setting. Not only are our actions viewed, but our feelings, inner reasoning, beliefs, and held positions come into view as well. A wealth of information becomes available to us. (The two-way arrow has also been referred to as "double arrow attention," as taught by G.I. Gurdjieff and referred to by P.D. Ouspensky, where an awareness of subject and object is held simultaneously.) (9)

EXERCISE 5:
Two-way Arrow

> Practice the two-way-arrow method of observing with intention. Select a time, for a half-hour, where you call to mind the exercise and try to hold the two-way observation for a few seconds. As you stray from the task you set for yourself, gently bring the attention back—no judgment, no complaint. Just try again. Stay with this effort for the half-hour chosen. If you lose the thread and don't remember until hours later, no problem. When you wish, set another half-hour for yourself. Stop at the end of each half-hour you set for yourself and take a break before starting again.
>
> This is not an easy task. It is actually quite difficult to do successfully for more than a second or two at a time. One great hurdle is the human tendency to get absorbed into each moment and lose connection with our thoughts and feelings. Between reactions, desires, and imagination, there is little of our attention left to use for clear observation. Clear, two-way observation is the task. A sense of our selves engaged in the moment is the aim.

Success can be quite subtle at first, but eventually, sudden moments of insight are likely to occur. Change will not happen overnight. Time and serious effort are needed. There is much to learn and much to gain—with pitfalls and rewards along the way. The beauty of this practice is that it can be done anywhere and at any time—whenever we remember to do so, whenever we awake. Any progress we make along the way will directly enhance our teacher-effectiveness in developing settings so that they will not contribute to anger, and in addressing highly-charged incidents that arise.

PERSPECTIVE:

Every person collects and develops multiple perspectives as a life is lived. These perspectives may be developed intentionally by the individual or be a result of accident and circumstance (the far more common occurrence). Perspectives may also be formed in an individual through the intention of others, with benevolence or self-interest being the primary intent. A scale (in schools) as such, might run at one end from the providing of a rich learning environment where students get to explore and develop their strengths and passions, to extreme mind-control and brainwashing at the other end. Schools have existed for centuries across this entire gamut.

As teachers, an awareness of the perspectives we hold is of extreme importance, as our perspectives will color and guide all of what we see and what we do. This, in turn, will affect the experience of every student in our charge. The clearer we are in our vision, the more able we become in our action.

Then there exists the possibility for teachers (and every person) to effect change in their own collection/complex of perspectives. This is key. Not only do the views we hold get exposed to light, but we become agents for change in ourselves. We have more ability to encourage or discourage the perspectives that we discover in ourselves. We create a better teacher.

This entire effort on the part of teachers is substantial, yet is comprised of continued, small efforts over a significant amount of time. We might watch ourselves grow, as we could watch a tree grow, over time—and as the Chinese proverb goes:

"When is the best time to plant a tree?"
"Ten years ago."
"When is the next best time to plant a tree?"
"Today!"

END-OF-CHAPTER QUESTIONS:

1. Can perspective be changed in a student? In a teacher? In anyone?
2. In general, can a broader, deeper perspective be cultivated in a person? How?
3. How can we tell if a perspective we hold is helping or hurting our efforts?
4. How do we proceed when we don't know what will work in a specific situation? How might perspective be involved?
5. Why might the concept of "Small change. Major impact!" (Peter) be so effective at times?
6. What might be the value of watching movies with heroic teachers, as mentioned above?
7. Does the concept of *Two-Way Arrow* resonate with you? In what ways? Have you already held a sense of this in some manner?

CHAPTER THREE

SAFETY

"Do not do to others what angers you if done to you by others."
—**Socrates**

SAFE ENVIRONMENT:

The first priority in any classroom is safety for all. I have more than once told students, as individuals or as a class, that physical safety is a basic starting point in the classroom, followed by emotional safety. I let them know that my actions as *teacher* would reflect this priority. This second part, emotional safety, has led to some interesting class discussions, with questions coming up such as:

- What does emotional safety mean?
- What does it look like?
- How does it relate to us now in this classroom?
- How can we recognize something that is not safe for ourselves or others?

One of the obvious examples of a situation that is emotionally unsafe is bullying. The very intent of bullying is to make the recipient feel fearful, cowed, and emotionally unsafe. The intent is to establish a framework of power where most or all of the power shifts to one side, the bullying side. However, though bullying is usually done with clear awareness and intention, it may not always be so. There may be varying degrees of awareness on the part of the bully, and intentions might be muddled.

E.G. — DARIN: BULLY?

Darin, enrolled in a teacher-certification curriculum, was taking a college course in a foreign language. He described one particular class. The teacher called on him to stand in front of the class to recite work from a certain assignment. Darin had not been able to grasp the material enough to be able to do that and told the teacher so. The teacher either did not understand or did not accept this, and five minutes later asked of Darin the same task. Darin was no more ready for it at this point. When, a half-hour later, Darin was asked once more to come to the front of the room for the same task, he became angry. After class the teacher, who seemed genuinely baffled, asked him why he was angry. Darin explained.

This is a situation where the first request of this sort was reasonable. A second such request reflects either intention or ignorance on the part of the teacher. The third request becomes bullying, whether intentional or not.

Unintentional actions that fall short of bullying might fall under the category of simple ignorance or of *teasing*. Teasing may be done with intention to hurt, though often the awareness of how the teasing actually affects others is non-existent, which can make it a difficult concept to grasp about one's behavior. Writer and psychologist Dan Kindlon, for example, asked a small group of boys:

"'Does Teasing ever hurt?' Several boys admit that it does. 'Then how can you tell when you've hurt someone?'... More silence. They don't have a clue. They're not faking it to look cool or tough." (1)

Whether teasing is done with intention or without much thought on the part of the teaser, there is opportunity as well as responsibility on the part of the teacher to monitor and to engage where appropriate. The key here is to determine when teacher involvement is appropriate, and when it might fall into the realm of over-protection or interference.

The teacher might also act as a catalyst in bringing fruitful discussions to class, or to confer with individuals. Much can be said about the importance of helping students understand more about how their actions affect others and how the actions of others affect them. Much of what is presented in this book is directly or indirectly linked to the development of a richer self-understanding and inner life for all classroom participants—with the purpose of each individual gaining capacity in influencing his or her inner and outer environment.

Another example of an emotionally unsafe setting is when expectations and biases on the part of a teacher or peers negatively impacts a student's self-image or sense of self-worth, and consequently the willingness to attempt various activities and challenges. This could then negatively affect the student's school performance academically, socially, and more. A downward spiral ensues.

Bias and negative expectation can be nurtured through intention, ignorance, or carelessness. The results will generally be the same for the receiving party, but the possibility of amelioration of the difficulty will vary for the person holding the bias or negative attitude.

It is the responsibility of every teacher to look earnestly at these traces of his own negative positions or rigid perspectives and work to change them. If a teacher does not have the ability or inclination to do so she/he should leave the teaching profession. A casual or careless attitude toward the wellbeing of students on the part of a teacher does not belong in the classroom. Each student deserves a chance to perform based on his own merits without the added weight of bias and/or bullying.

A NOTE ON CYBER-BULLYING:

Cyber-bullying has become an easy, *prevalent*, serious form of bullying which holds some particularly insidious traits. This is a form of bullying that can be witnessed by many, made public in a large way. The perpetrator of cyber-bullying can, as well, feel a protective sense of distance from and feelings for the person targeted. Then, perhaps the most frightening part, is the sense of protection from immediate repercussions a bully might feel by being at a physical distance and/or operating through the online creation of an avatar. Similar to the theme of *the savage* in William Golding's *The Lord of the Flies*, the *mask* (like a computer) allowed Jack to hide and be immune from the *laws of civilization*, allowing brutality and anarchy to flourish.

Of Jack painting his face: "He looked in astonishment, no longer at himself, but at an awesome stranger. He ... leapt to his feet, laughing excitedly. ...His sinewy body held up a mask that drew their eyes and appalled them. He began to dance and his laughter became a bloodthirsty snarling. ... and the mask was a thing of its own, behind which Jack hid, liberated from shame and self-consciousness." (2)

The work of the teacher is to make clear, intimately and immediately clear, that there are human beings involved in all parts of any form of bullying—that dangers lurk for all parties involved, and the use of technology does not make it all a game.

HOW TO FALL:

One of the first things a child needs to learn in order to be safe is how to fall safely. We all will fall, in a surprising variety of ways. If we fall safely from wherever it is, we can get right back into action, or at least minimize any recuperative time, physically or emotionally. Consider these possible ways to fall:

- A baby tries to walk but falls on her diaper; she gets right up and tries again.
- A boy is running in the woods and trips; he lands in a way that does not snap a (human) limb.
- A woman speeds down a slope on a snowboard, pushing her limits, and falls more than once; she gets back up for more.
- A man experiences disappointments while teaching; he skirts disillusionment and forges ahead.
- A hiker steps on a root in the trail and rolls with the movement, instantly shifting weight to the other foot; no ankle injury ensues.
- A teacher feels far from the embodiment of the heroic teacher of films; she takes steps forward, creating herself in the image of what she wishes to be, not oppressed by the chasm.

The question then arises of how a teacher is to provide a safe environment—yet one that does not simultaneously squelch risk-taking. A balance must be sought. If students were to gain safety at all costs—and never have the opportunity to *take their measure*, to test their limits—it would be a great loss for them and for society. One engaging book for young readers (and old) that beautifully portrays this particular struggle for balance is *The Giver* by Lois Lowry. (3)

Let's consider ourselves first as teachers. How do we fall? How do we get back up? How can we avoid falling at certain times and accept the possibility at other times?

E.G. — GLENN

It was early on in Glenn's work with Head Start and in his teaching career. Working with four-year-olds was a joy, for them and for Glenn, though it was not all sweet and easy. The nature of Head Start was that children with the most critical need in a community were selected for the program so that they could be provided needed support in order to have a somewhat equal chance of success in school. Children selected might live on a farm without siblings, and consequently see no other children for an entire week—or live in a trailer with six siblings—or live in a setting where discipline was thought to be more important than nurturing.

At the end of each school day the children went back to their homes. When some of the students left for home Glenn felt a heaviness in his heart. He knew what some of them were returning to. It began to drain his energy and become an added weight to carry, making the teaching day less fluid, less rich for the children. He had to make a separation. Glenn realized this and made a conscious decision: *When the children are with me they are mine for the day. When they leave on the bus they are the responsibility of others. I will let go of the responsibility and the vulnerability I feel that goes along with it.*

The desired effects did come about, though all responsibility for the teachers did not vanish after the school bell rang. They would always need to watch out for the wellbeing of each child, monitoring their physical and emotional safety. In addition, a nationwide aim of the program was to work with families to help enrich the home experience of each child. Visits to the home by Head Start staff were a regular ingredient in this effort.

Any teacher who returns to work with a net loss of energy from the previous day, on any kind of regular basis, for any reason, is not destined to be a teacher for long. Irritation, fatigue, impatience, and anger will be the likely results. This would then be disastrous for both teacher and student, a lose-lose situation. This type of "fall" leads to the inability to function well in the school setting.

Another way to *fall down* is to *fall short*. An example of this was presented in Chapter Two when discussing the divide between the heroic teacher of film and the teacher toiling in the trenches every day. Yes, there will be days when the classroom "dance" will be more difficult than on other days. Yes, there will be days of discouragement and perhaps even contemplation of giving up. What then does *getting back up* look like? First is to simply recognize the truth of these statements. *There will be days like this...*

What then? We continue—we look to improve. Without an effort at moving forward the likely trend will be to slide backwards. Maintaining status quo is difficult to do for long periods of time, and can get dull. The potential next move is toward negativity in various of its many faces.

We might *fall short* in a number of ways. The image we have of ourselves will take many forms as settings change and as the *hat* we wear changes. From father, to sister, to friend, to grandmother—we, as teachers, have numerous roles to play in and out of school. And the question still comes, "What do we do when we don't stack up (to the image we want)?" One thing I can say is that anyone who is reading this text and making any effort with exercises or suggestions presented, is taking concrete steps toward the ideal image they hold— forging forward. Appreciate progress, at any pace, to any degree.

EXERCISE 6:
Taking Action

- Observe your current state, your position in relation to where you would like to be as a teacher.
- Accept this observation and your position without undue self-criticism or judgement. Practice **impartial self-observation** (an extremely valuable tool).
- Determine or identify some of your goals or targets. (Some may be less visible or graspable at this point, and will form as you make efforts with this exercise.)
- Find some way to practice, to move toward your goals. (A small effort practiced over years can be clearly productive, and can strengthen perseverance and will along the way.)
- Keep getting up and trying again after every time you fall/fail.

- Let go of the negative connotations around **fall** and **fail**. These are experiences and tools, not finished products.

It is said that Thomas Edison viewed each failure he encountered with appreciation—taking him one step closer to his target—one more failure out of the way.

E.G. — JASON AND GLENN

In this non-traditional classroom setting our friend Darcy was teaching Jason and me the fine-art of technical rock-climbing. Like two little ducklings we would follow her all over the rock faces in New Paltz/Gardner, NY, at "the Gunks" (as the bedrock Shawangunk Ridge is affectionately known to climbers, hikers, and Hudson Valley locals and visitors). It was exciting and scary, though actually quite safe, as Darcy made sure we followed the technical protocol for this sport.

At a certain point toward the end of our first season, I turned to Jason and said, "We've been steadily improving at climbing, but if we want to seriously improve, to pick up the pace, I think we need to be ready to fall." We had stayed within a "safe zone" where we did not fall while climbing, but there was yet another safe-zone, where we could actually start falling and still be safe. Jason agreed. We had Darcy start taking us on climbs that were just beyond our current climbing-ability range. It worked. We fell. We quickly improved as we kept reaching into the next level of climbing difficulty. We had also reached a new level of exciting.

KEEPING RECORD:

A very different type of safety for teachers comes in the form of written records. We'll look at two aspects of this here—Note-taking and Record-keeping.

NOTE-TAKING:

One of the simplest and strongest tools that a teacher has at his fingertips is *note-taking*. As a companion with *observation* this dual-tool is the bedrock of a teacher's (or anyone's) ability to *assess* and *adapt* in the classroom or in any setting working with students—making change and growth available to all participants.

NOTE-TAKING AS AN ASSESSMENT TOOL:

The Head Start program I worked with was located in northern New York. Our primary goal there was to provide a safe, rich setting for the four-year-old children who attended class. We had two classrooms of fifteen students each and were fortunate to have a large space to work with in the basement of the Methodist church in town. We would create up to a dozen separate locations, separated by low walls, featuring such interest-areas as: *blocks, water-play, dress-up clothes, sand-play, quiet area with many pillows, cooking area, trucks and cars area, library, art,* and more. A theme would then be woven through the interest areas, such as *Working in Teams* or *Spring Growth*, and was changed every three weeks.

The incidental learning (learning through one's environment, as compared to direct instruction) was strong, as was the intentional learning integrated into it, such as studying letters through play or learning to dress for various weathers. What brought all of this together was the effort the staff made to monitor the flow of traffic in each interest-room, make observations of individual students, and record their personal observations. Were some areas crowded while other areas lay vacant? Did particular students spend nearly all of their time in one area or follow one particular student wherever she went? Were there students who avoided any area that had other children in it? What language development issues were noticed? An unlimited variety of questions and observations might arise and become fodder for the next teacher planning session.

Recording observations of this sort was an essential part of this process and helped teachers decide what to do next to maintain or to change momentum in the classroom. It produced information useful in planning for individual students. Recording notes about student comments, actions, or interactions also allowed a teacher to mentally let go of any of these observations that he was trying to remember. He would instead be able to refer back to his notes. His mind would be clear for the next observation to come. It's difficult to overemphasize the importance of this fact. The sooner that notes are recorded, the fresher they will be, and the fresher the mind will be that can let the memory rest—task completed.

Too often, however, note-taking is treated casually—approached as if it had little value, or as a nuisance. Effectiveness plummets. For example, when something significant is noticed by the teacher and she puts off recording it—saying to herself, I will write this down when I get a moment—too often the observation is either forgotten, seems to lose its value, or important aspects of the observation are lost. Only occasionally can this "waiting" method be successful. It can be far more effective to keep a notepad or small notebook handy at all times so that a quick note can be jotted down. The recording doesn't need to be in-depth note-taking and is better if it isn't. But capturing the most salient aspects of an exchange, behavior, or teacher-insight can provide the groundwork for expanded notes later.

EXERCISE 7:
Writing Notes—Memory Link

> To compare immediate "real-time note-taking" with "later-in-the-day note-taking" try this. Set a habit of writing shorthand detailed notes on a single, selected event occurring in the classroom (or at home), each day—not full-sentence descriptions; rather, words and phrases that you think will be sufficient to jog your memory of the fuller details later on. Do this daily for two weeks.

SAFETY

This "comparison" exercise has two parts:

Method 1—Write and Review

Jot down notes about incidents or insights during the day as soon after they occur as possible. Later in the day practice recalling the earlier event you had taken notes on, and the details surrounding it. Then check what you have written to compare the thoroughness of your recall.

[This will not, however, give a completely accurate comparison to the later-in-the-day note-taking method described below, as it is highly likely that what you remember will be enhanced by writing down the notes earlier, adding a strong form of learning to your effort-kinesthetic learning* (learning through movement). You will also have the added strength of the focus you used to zero in on your topic and write about it. You may still, however, find useful insight when comparing this to the next method presented here.]

Method 2—Late-day Write

In the following week engage in this exercise, but wait until later in the day to record notes on your earlier observations. Set your intention when an event occurs, to recall it hours later, but write nothing down at the time.

What difference do you notice, regarding how it felt and in the notes themselves? Do you feel that over the course of only a few hours, the strength of memory can weaken or become cloudy? Was there a qualitative difference in the notes themselves—a difference in content, detail, or accuracy, when comparing to Method 1 above? Have some events you wished to recall totally slipped your memory until some far later time? Has their importance seemed to fade?

*Multi-sensory approaches to learning will include kinesthetic learning to help the learning become deep-seated in the individual. This is a common best-practice, at any age, for student or teacher. The kinesthetic aspect can be accomplished in a number of ways (a young student, for example, might repeat the alphabet while jumping on a trampoline), though writing is a common channel for this. It is simple, easy, and can have highly beneficial and direct results.

ANECDOTAL NOTE-TAKING:

—is a form based on unofficial, unscientific observation. It's about recording what the observer sees in a narrative manner, similar to the telling of a story.

Definition—Oxford English Dictionary (OED):
anecdotal notes. Small narrative incidents. 4

Definition—Dictionary.com:
anecdotal notes. Based on personal observation, case study reports, or random investigations rather than systematic scientific evaluation. 5

This does not, however, mean that *anything goes* in the recording of notes. There are methods and material that would not be appropriate for anecdotal notes. More on this to follow:

The taking of *anecdotal notes* is different from *record-keeping* notes that will be discussed in the following section. The notes referred to here are meant to inform the teacher and to help her be accurate in her recall. I have at times been surprised looking back at notes I had written about a particular student, noticing that there had been striking changes in the student over the period of a year, changes that had come about slowly. (I've used this for long-term, multi-year tutoring students as well.)

Referring to anecdotal records I've been able to clearly relay to parents what I based some of my statements and decisions on concerning their child. I've developed learning strategies and interventions that were strengthened by the notes I had taken. All aspects of the teaching process can be enhanced when the teacher holds a bounty of related information to work with.

There is another area of concern that teachers might need to address, another area concerning safety—the occasional need to defend, legally or otherwise, certain actions taken, whether academic or discipline-related. Parental anger or the threat of a law suit from any party can be very uncomfortable. Having clear notes allows the teacher to state a case simply and objectively, incorporating less personal judgment, defensive positioning, and reactive anger. Strength can replace whining. Presenting supporting data will usually make teacher actions more easily accepted by parents, and parents may have a clearer picture of their child. The enriched parent-teacher communication and understanding possible at this point would more likely translate to enhanced programming for the student, the ultimate goal here.

Impending official actions against a teacher can be another area of concern. If administrative actions are being contemplated, then record-keeping (including anecdotal notes) might help clarify the teacher's position and present a much stronger case, making it easier to find a mutually acceptable solution to a problem or to clarify a misperception.

In terms of privacy, legality, and policy regarding personal teacher-notes, it's important for each teacher to check with his administration. As I understand it, such notes taken belong solely to the teacher; other supervisory personnel such as administration may keep their own notes if they wish. The notes are there entirely for the purpose of bettering the teacher's own performance in the classroom and with students, hence the reason for their protection. They do not belong to the school and they are not for public record. They will not follow the student. Yet policies may differ from state to state. Investigate.

Additionally, as the use of electronic notes and information is more widely employed at all levels of education, new precautions must be taken. Kerry Gallagher, Terry Magid, and Kobie Pruitt present a useful overview in the article "The Educator's Guide to Student Data Privacy" published on the site *ConnectSafely.org*. We observe this statement from the article, "Teachers are ethically obliged to follow and model good digital citizenship practices and behaviors with their students. This includes thinking carefully about the digital products and processes that are incorporated in any project or lesson design." (6) They go on to offer specific pointers regarding recorded information and more.

This all points to the need for taking serious consideration of what is written—always, anywhere. We all know how easy it is to find electronic communications made public in a very big way. I recall one parent saying to her child, "Whenever you write any email or text, imagine seeing it broadcast to the world on a large screen in the middle of Times Square. It could easily happen." Her words appear prophetic at this point in our culture.

Another important concern is note-taking content. In regards to the subjective/objective question, consider the difference between writing, "Davey was very angry at lunch-time today," and, "At lunch period Davey picked up a chair and threw it across the room, then screamed loudly." The latter is simply an observed fact. The former is filtered through the teacher's judgement. Accurate or not, judgement can be more easily argued with and challenged by others than an observed fact—and more difficult for the teacher to defend. A teacher-note such as, "Sally seems tired today," is fine as long as it is made clear that it is a qualified statement. Here the qualifying word is "seems." It would then be good to support the statement with something like, "She several times put her head down on her arms and closed her eyes."

Time will be an argument used by many teachers to express the impossibility of actually taking notes during a school day, and *time* for teachers certainly is an issue. But find a way. Create the habit of taking notes. Make the effort to do it quietly rather than blatantly run over to a notebook as soon as something particular happens. This could embarrass a student or create mistrust or anxiety in the classroom. Yet, generally, to see a teacher taking notes is not at all an odd thing. When working one-to-one or in small groups with students I've occasionally been asked by a student what I was doing when I wrote down something I had observed. Depending on the age level I might answer: trying to become a better teacher, assisting my memory, or keeping track of things that I think can be valuable and help the class. This is usually all that's needed—and I am at the same time being truthful. Students sense that.

Several other benefits can come from the effort of recording information. Writing down observations can cause things to become clearer as I struggle for accuracy in my recording. I might also find it easier to refrain from making inaccurate, vague, or exaggerated emotional statements in later discussions (which may be of significant value) by having specific notes to refer to and by having practiced being accurate. There also exists the possibility of going back to one or more of the parties involved in an incident for clarification and to point out statements they had made. This could help jog their memory (and mine) and promote further useful information. If a teacher were to quote an individual incorrectly, or if such a teacher statement was disputed by a student, the result could be loss of trust, disrespect, or anger. A record can circumvent much of this.

Through taking notes I also get to learn about my own personal dealings with anger. Anecdotal notes about my personal exchanges and encounters with anger and what I see in myself can be of immense value. (I would suggest keeping these notes in a separate notebook because they don't directly relate to student or class issues.) I can learn about anger by seeing how others interchange with anger and placing myself in their shoes. I can observe my own reactions and responses. Then hopefully I'll notice when I personally become a factor in contributing to highly emotional events or in helping alleviate the tension in them.

Kinesthetic action (as described above) comes into play, as well, when writing or typing is involved. This supports a multi-sensory approach to learning. It works for teachers, as well as for students—and hooray for teacher learning! How else can we keep a classroom vibrant and exciting?

E.G. — ASHER

Recently on a road trip with one of my grandsons (a nine-year-old) we found ourselves deep in a heated discussion about the meaning of different words and the power that each word can hold. I remember discussing the subtle and not-so-subtle differences between "assertive drivers" and "aggressive drivers" and the meanings of the words we used to support our arguments. It went on for a while.

"People can argue about any word, even the word 'the,'" Asher said.

I agreed and spoke about the difference in the terms "The Facebook" and "Facebook"—the difference between a *coffee-table edition* and a *way of life*—vast.

We entered several other highly interesting areas regarding words. I brought up a discussion he and I had had when he was five years old, after a visit to the Museum of Natural History. He was enthusiastically telling me about the tyrant lizard he saw there, the Tyrannosaurus Rex.

"The biggest lizard," he said.

"Then would the Maple tree in that field be called a Tyrant Tree?" I asked. We continued the thread—"Or a Tyrant Dad?" I added, (who was driving).

"Or a Tyrant Grandma?" he said, and we all laughed.

We went on this way for a bit until I stopped him in his tracks as a five-year-old with, "How about a Tyrant Idea?" He immediately became quiet, sitting in his car seat in the back, and I could practically see the gears turning madly in his mind—each gear making a new link to the next...

As we drove along, returning from Canada nearly twice his lifetime later, he recalled all of this happening years earlier, and it entered into our current conversation. At one point in the middle of a heated yet cogent period of argument stressing the ideas we were trying to grasp, Asher stopped and said as an aside, "I love doing this," and then leapt back into our discussion. I laughed.

Two days later, I tried to recall what had started that conversation. It had seemed as though he had leapt up several levels of maturity as we conversed, and I was trying to see what might have sparked it. I could not. I knew that the energy that we had built up through two-and-a-half weeks of camping and hiking together through Maine and Nova Scotia was significant, an essential ingredient—but what was the visible spark, and was there one? A week later I found it. I was able to locate a small post-it note that I had jotted a few words on at the end of this marathon late-night drive home after weeks away. There I found the beginning of the conversation, obscure though it was. I had forgotten it.

During a quiet moment sitting in the passenger seat, Asher had asked, "When you think to yourself, do you think in your own voice?" I paused for a time, and then started our conversation rolling again, just as we were rolling along at 9:00 p.m., the beginning of a six-hour push for home (having just stepped off of a ten-hour ferry ride). I was not in a teacher-student position with my grandson, but I was glad I had written the note and was able to see the spark that ignited our very fertile discussion. Such simple observations can help us catch a glimpse into the thinking of students—and grandchildren.

Better understanding students in a class will help a teacher know how to address the students' specific needs, anxieties, frustrations, and hot-spots. Though the story above is not one about anger or the classroom, it illustrates the accuracy and value to be found in the exercise of note-taking. Such an effort can greatly enhance a teacher's behavior-management skills, and help especially in avoiding the need for behavioral management tactics at all.

WHAT TO RECORD—A SAMPLE:

General—
- Observe myself as well as my students. (What works and what doesn't toward my goals in the classroom?)

- Am I angered at certain occurrences?
- Am I aware of my participation and contribution in classroom events—physically, mentally, and emotionally?
- Describe student's interaction with peers.
- Does the child play alone or with others?
- Is the observed behavior different or new for this student?
- Note time of day and associated events when an incident occurs. Any patterns to be seen?
- Note the chaos level in the room. How does the behavior of students change at these moments?
- Does structure or discipline in the classroom seem to break down during transition times?
- For progress-monitoring, frequent notes across targeted settings or a broad spectrum of settings is useful. Could social performance be affecting academic performance, or vice-versa?
- What appears to be the student's main interests?

In regards to anger—
- Observe hot-spots.
- What is my role as teacher in these moments?
- Do some students trigger my temper more than others? Can I see any reasons for this? Valid reasons?
- Note what might set a student off.
- Describe the scene and actions around a hot event, including as much relevant information as possible. What is it that precedes angry episodes for specific students (Antecedent)? Describe what the behavior looks like (Behavior). What is it that follows an angry moment (Consequence)? This is the ABC approach.
- Note behaviors that are repetitive, provocative, anti-social, teasing, bullying, self-injurious—anything that can bring harm to any individual or to class-functioning.

Review and further note:
- Be as objective as possible without infusing the observation with

personal opinion. If you do make a judgment call in some way, include support data—why, when, where, how, which links .... Describe an action. ("His face turned red and was scrunched-up tight," rather than "He was angry.")
- Discussions with students after an incident can hold more value if specific observations can be brought into the conversation, ones that have an impartial feel to them (objective note-taking).
- Be ready to hear your observation spoken publicly. (Even though it's unlikely, it's a good guideline, so take care when writing.)
- Memory is known to change with time (even over a few minutes), so the earlier the notes can be written down, the better.
- Keep a clear timeline with notes taken. Date all notes and any reference to something from a different time. ("He mentioned an argument with ___ last Friday, March 10th.")
- Having a vague sense of wishing to write notes is not enough. Intention is needed—strong intention to make it happen.
- Store notes in a secure location, for teacher-use only.
- Record positive observations along with all the rest. Have these available to present to parents and others, both to present a balanced picture of the student and to ease parent acceptance of critical information—as well as to help yourself as teacher to focus on student strengths.
- Keep notes brief and to the point, yet include enough related data to be clear and useful.

Add your own observation categories to these lists.

RECORD-KEEPING:

Record keeping is the more formal side of note-taking. Requirements for record-keeping may come from individual schools, districts, or state and federal government. There are many regulations concerning what records must be kept, by whom, in what form, and who has access to them. Numerous legal cases have occurred regarding who has the right to see or obtain copies of official records held by schools, and rights are now established for parents, schools, and the individual students themselves. *"Student education records are official and confidential documents protected by one of the nation's strongest privacy protection laws, the Family Educational Rights and Privacy Act (FERPA)... also known as the Buckley Amendment. FERPA gives parents (as well as students in post-secondary schools) the right to review and confirm the accuracy of education records. This and other United States "privacy" laws ensure that information about citizens collected by schools and government agencies can be released only for specific and legally defined purposes."* IES-NCES (Institute of Education Sciences/National Center for Education Statistics), March 1997. (7)

The policies of each school in regards to this should be part of the orientation for any new teacher at the school. But if this is not made clear, it would be wise for any teacher new to a school district to ask for particulars. Much is at stake for all parties involved. This is especially true for special education teachers where regulations have become more numerous and strident. IEP (Individual Educational Plan) regulations, for example, are very clear about steps and stages and the appropriate time-line to go with them.

Record-keeping is not an area for this book to cover in depth. Much information is available from many sources. The goal here is to distinguish formal record-keeping from anecdotal note-taking and to emphasize the importance of addressing record-keeping for the setting you enter. A second goal is to note the link between these two forms of gathering observational information. Informal note-taking can greatly enhance a teacher's effectiveness in record-keeping, such as with implementing IEP goals. Below are further notes on note-taking relating directly to record-keeping. What is valuable for one mode will enhance the other as well. Providing the best education for individual students will be a result of careful attention to this formal/informal duo.

EXERCISE 8:

House Rules

If you currently work in a school or any program involving students or clients, research or review policies governing anecdotal note-taking and the more formal record-keeping. First, however, I suggest that the reader who is unfamiliar with the complete set of rules for that school write down categories he thinks will be addressed in the rules/regulations/policies. Then write down what he thinks each category will cover. This practice will help set information that is uncovered, shed some light on assumptions that he might personally carry, and be fun. It will also be wise to know well the parameters and guidelines for the position held.

WHAT **NOT** TO WRITE:

- We have spoken of being aware of subjective statements made during note-taking. The more we include our opinion, the weaker the notes might become—unless we can clearly back up our statements, not only to the level of *our* satisfaction, but to that of others as well.
- Be aware of the legal implications of what is written in a student's records. If we are suspicious, for example, of a student's use of an illegal substance, a formal record may not be the best place to record this. For one thing, a suspicion differs considerably from a fact, and anything we include in a formal record will remain there, available for others to see—even years later.

Anything that is written into a student's records must be carefully assessed by the party writing the note (teacher, counselor, etc.). It could be valuable to consult with a peer or administrator regarding such information before recording it, or to find a different avenue of communication.

- Consider also that there are some statements that might require follow-up, by the teacher, student, parent, other agency, or body of law. Consider what will be set in motion by formal statements made.

END-OF-CHAPTER QUESTIONS:

1. What other specific areas of "safety" are of concern for you in a classroom?
2. What do other teachers around you do for note-taking or record-keeping? Ask. And what related issues have they been faced with?
3. Can you recall an interaction with a parent or administrator where it might have been to your advantage to have supportive notes to back you up? Describe.
4. Have there been interesting bits of conversation you have had with children, yours or others', that you would like to recall now?
5. Where do you employ note-taking now—shopping lists, to-do lists, journal keeping? Is the purpose of each clear?
6. How could the practices you already use aid you in classroom note-taking skills?
7. Can you see other areas of concern regarding note-taking?
8. In the memory/note-taking exercise, as the effort to write notes during the day while teaching becomes established in you, does it become easier or more difficult as the days progress? How?

CHAPTER FOUR

ANGER TOOLS

"Anybody can become angry—that is easy, but to be angry with the right person and to the right degree and at the right time and for the right purpose, and in the right way—that is not within everybody's power and is not easy."
—**Aristotle**

THE TEACHER AS A CLASSROOM TOOL:

It may seem odd to refer to a teacher as a tool, but if you think of the function and purpose of a teacher, and the effort that goes into developing and shaping that functioning in the classroom, the reference to a tool may not appear so out of place. The purpose of teacher-training schools is to develop teachers to perform in a classroom in a satisfactory manner and to understand how to continuously fine-tune themselves in regards to this manner. A teacher has an assigned job—a tool has an assigned job. Both are capable of functioning in varied settings and for varied purposes; of course, only one can change or enhance its own functioning, for only one has the will to do so. Will is a powerful thing.

We can decide to do something—and then do it. It materializes. At least we are designed this way, whether we are able to execute or not. This is an extraordinary gift—one that we might continuously invoke as we strive to improve as a teacher and classroom conductor.

In this case, the tool (teacher) is not an inanimate object that has no function when it is not at work, nor is it an automaton that is preprogrammed and preset (we hope). The teacher is capable of, and tasked with, developing as someone who can consider multiple aspects of student needs, classroom management, documentation, student growth, and more. A teacher need also attend to her own growth and development as a teacher, so that all might benefit as she moves toward veteran teacher status. This describes a tool that improves with time.

Though certainly not confined to the teaching profession, the personal development of a teacher has far-ranging implications. As a teacher stands in front of a classroom full of students he will set an example to those students on how to act and to think. Whether students reject or emulate a teacher, they will be influenced. Whether a teacher is deeply aware of this position or oblivious, his influence will still be there.

We might begin to see then the importance of becoming a tool, an instrument of awareness. Only in this way can a teacher present intentional influence to students, rather than accidental influence. Only in this way can a teacher not only develop herself as a person in chosen ways, but also be able to pass this information and understanding on to her students. For students to be able to direct their own growth and development will be a strength that will be forever valuable to them—one of the primary accomplishments of their teacher.

TEACHER AS THE HOLDER OF POSITION

In any classroom the teacher holds a unique position, and is expected to do so. In several sections of this book we'll see evidence of ways in which this is so—from educator, to confidant, to disciplinarian. We will continue to explore, throughout these pages, the many aspects of teaching that can lead away from resistance, frustration, and anger in the classroom—and instead build strong connections, a trusting environment, and interest in being present in school.

Another theme we are following is that of knowing when to lean more toward objectivity or more toward subjectivity when relating to students. When shall we as teachers *lean in close* or *stand off* and hold the position of official rule? Exercises within are geared toward discovering our best position with this in varied classroom settings and scenarios. One teacher whom I greatly admire has a bit of insight on this for us.

> *"I have discovered one small piece of technique never so far encountered in a book. It is this. It is much more efficient to refer to yourself in the third person as 'the teacher' than it is to say 'I' or 'me.' To say, 'When you hear me call you must come back,' doesn't carry as much weight as, 'When the teacher calls you must come back.' It seems the impersonal 'teacher' does not evoke the same feelings of restraint and resistance. The child feels freer. As a rule children want to conform but they unconsciously resent the personal touch. I think most of us do if we only knew it."*
> —A. L. Staveley (1)

In Chapter Three, when I told students of my responsibility for safety in the classroom and how I would enforce this, I was speaking in the manner described above. I was filling a role that I was given and that I accepted. I would enforce what was needed to provide safety for all. I was playing the role of the teacher, setting personal feelings aside.

ROLE MODEL

Though teachers may be looked up to as superhuman by some students and subhuman by other students, they are, like other humans, *human*. Teachers generally experience the same range of emotions and stresses and grace and challenges. Since teachers are role-models for children and young adults each day, and help guide them in their growth, it's of the utmost importance that this is not done carelessly or even casually.

Too much is at stake. The uniqueness of each teacher is an essential thing and important to preserve, yet there are some traits and tendencies common to the world of teachers that might best be starved or curbed, while others are nourished and strengthened.

Students will always note something about the teacher standing in front of them. Will they see someone who is imbued with care, or carelessness—one who makes efforts to deliver a strong curriculum, or just try to get by? Will they find before them a person who can inspire them to live according to held principles, or someone who seems distant or pushes them away from the education effort? There are many scales or spectrums upon which teachers can rate themselves. We have just mentioned a few. The effort alone of observing and rating oneself can provide valuable insight into one's teaching strengths and areas to improve upon. What the students *see* will also hold value.

If I can, for example, model for my students how to diffuse, side-step, or engage anger that knocks against me; then they can see me being calm, holding strength, and managing a worthy adversary. This is education in a real way. This is how learning can be deeply experienced. This is how the strength of the teacher can be felt and incorporated into the lives of the students and how students can learn to do what they see and sense as appropriate.

I emphasize here once again the value of intention. Intention can help set us toward our goals, free us from major distractions, and provide motivation to keep moving as we choose. Yet, it must be accompanied with action—proper action—or we might simply send ourselves around in circles or off into la-la-land. Moving with intention is one of the themes of this book—with the purpose of developing able, caring, effective teachers/human beings. I can recall a few teachers I've had like this in my educational experience. They stand out for me. They inspire me—still, decades later.

EXERCISE 9:
The Teacher's Role

List aspects of the role you are to play in the classroom. This might contain:

- a list of expected duties and responsibilities (job description)
- additional duties and responsibilities that you feel are essential
- unexpected roles you have already been called upon to perform
- less tangible goals, such as: interest, empathy, compassion, and determination
- goals of an even more subtle nature, such as: self-possession and self-awareness
- goal-setting and actualizing

Review and add to this list periodically.

We now observe a selection of specific tools that are essential to quality teaching, connecting with students, and addressing anger and other hot-spots in the classroom.

OBSERVATION:

Observation is a bedrock tool. It is intricately entwined with the use of other tools, with action, and with growth. The growth of observational skill parallels the growth of a baby, a teacher, a wizened elder. Along this progression we see, embedded within the observation, awareness. As this awareness increases, so does the strength of observation—a process that might continue for a lifetime. A person who is actually able to maintain such growth may offset many symptoms of a failing mind, be of great use to family and community around her, and experience increasing joy with age.

The period along this spectrum that we explore here, however, is that of the teacher. There is much to say and much that cannot be said in words, regarding observation. Presented here are aspects of observation that might be of use to anyone who is intentionally exploring the skill of observation, development as a teacher, and development as a person.

- As we look at something, *Observing* it and *thinking* about it are very different activities—with vastly different results. We use different parts of the brain for these activities. The former can be far more direct and accurate in terms of gathering data. While a thinking mind is needed, it's easy to complicate observation by passing all data through layers of thinking about what is being observed—coloring it without being aware of doing so.

- Observation has to do with facts—making note of *what is* versus what we might *perceive* it is, or *wish* it is (or isn't)—without sending the information through a matrix of personal attractions and repulsions.

- Recording observations immediately will preserve their fresh quality. Waiting to write notes brings in an unpredictable quality—memory.

- The observation that will be the most useful for our purposes here is *conscious observation*. This is observation of an event as it occurs and when we are simultaneously aware that we are observing. In this way we have the opportunity to determine our level of objectivity or investment in how the event looks—to see how we might be coloring what is seen. This is a capacity that takes serious effort to develop, not something that we can simply turn on as we wish, especially for the more subtle levels.

E.G. — MIDDLE SCHOOL

I recall, when in grade school, how some children were mercilessly teased because they were different than others. A great struggle took place within me. I wanted on one hand to be part of the "in-crowd," who are often the perpetrators of said inflictions—while at the same time I felt pain for the teased. "How am I so different from this teased person?" I would think. And I would conclude, "I have my own differences. How terrible it would feel for me, and does for this person now." I knew nothing about observing objectively, at least not by name, but I was able to experience some degree of awareness of myself in the middle of these tugging, conflicting emotions.

The experience remained difficult because I didn't know where to place value or how to act, though I could eventually see that the empathy alive in me seemed to carry the most weight in an objective sense. Wanting to be part of the clique was also a strong force, but clearly was directed by my own desires and self-interest. I consider myself fortunate to have had the strong, conflicting voices internally active in me at times, (though I didn't always welcome them). I would later learn to further develop this ability to look at multiple sides of situations, and to be aware of personal preferences I might be carrying that were coloring my perceptions, exaggerating, minimizing, or morphing what was actually occurring.

We each begin with our own ability-level in this area. The starting-level doesn't matter. We each hold the potential to become stronger.

- Energy—is needed to observe well
- With practice—a clear shift in observational ability can be experienced and observed
- The activity of observation will not always be pleasant, especially when viewing unflattering things in oneself, and may bring up negativity. A danger might be giving in to the negativity and getting discouraged or angry, losing energy. Yet, opportunity opens!

E.G. — HOW I CONTRIBUTE

One day, while teaching a high school class I was having trouble connecting with the students and even at keeping the lessons moving along. The flow felt jerky and some students were showing irritation at various points during the morning. When I had a break I tried to assess what was at work here and found myself focusing on particular students who were needling other students, or simply seemed to be in a surly mood. I noticed my own state of agitation, as well, and began to self-complain about succumbing to the negativity in the classroom.

Yet, I kept looking and asking myself questions. The answer to one of these questions was able to shine light on the sequence of events. I looked for when my own uncomfortable feelings began, and the answer was: neither at the beginning of class, nor half-way through the class—rather, before stepping into the classroom. I had brought negativity to class with me. I could even backtrack through the pre-class morning and identify both physical and emotional contributions to my mildly negative state. And this state, though subtle, I am sure had much to do with the functioning of the class.

Whether the students had their own negativity or not, was not the primary issue. I knew that, when I was fit and ready, I could help lift many students out of dull or complaining moods and bring about a vibrant class. This morning my mood, at worst, spawned the difficult classroom atmosphere, or at best, was unable to help lift the classroom energy. Either way, I now had some new knowledge to work with. I looked forward to stepping back in when my turn came around.

I can make a negative self-observation positive by taking a particular stance: I accept the particular observation about myself as an example of a common human characteristic, and welcome the sight/insight as a *positive opportunity to change*. More, please!

EXERCISE 10:
To Strengthen Observational Skill

Working with physical habits is often a good way to begin the effort of strengthening observation skills. Choose something (there are thousands of possibilities) that you do daily that falls into the realm of habit. For example, notice the way you rise up from sitting in a chair. Unless we are injured, or some other unique factor has entered, this is not something we usually do with much awareness. It is "beneath our radar".

1. At first (for one day or two) simply observe the way you do this. Note whether you lead with your head, set your feet into motion, or favor the right or left side of your body. What do your arms do to further this process? You might even begin to notice how you use the muscles of your torso, front and back.
2. Then make the effort to change some part of this process. One simple change can make a difference in the entire procedure. But the goal here is to observe—to observe yourself and to be aware that you are observing yourself. The effort at making the small change is meant only to bring in some sharpness of focus. A bit more of our attention can be engaged and a clearer picture available.
3. Work with this habit for a while, a minimum of seven days practice for best results. See what you see. After a few days of effort you will likely notice a number of things in addition to those mentioned in step 1. For example, you may find that you don't remember to watch yourself rise until after you have already risen from the chair. Even remembering to notice rising, at the moment you are actually getting out of the chair, is an accomplishment. Then, after several days' effort, you may begin to notice your rising from a chair whether you make an effort to notice or not. This is part of

> the automatic habituation process for a human. You can see it in action. (What do you think the next stage after this might be?)
>
> Other possibilities for observation include using your non-dominant hand for particular activities; tilting your head slightly to the right side, then the left side, then back straight—on and off for an hour; or chewing your food at a slightly faster or slower pace than usual. Have fun while you practice.

PERSPECTIVE:

An essential ingredient in any effort at avoiding, dissipating, or managing anger in the classroom, is an awareness and engagement with perspective—perspective on the part of the teacher, the students, and the school (with both policy and overall temperament). Above in this text can be found an entire chapter on Perspective (Chapter Two). Chapter One also presents a number of ways to explore, interact with, and hopefully expand awareness of our relationship to the perspectives that we hold, as well as perspectives of our students.

Perspective is mentioned here again due to the importance of understanding the influence it has on all participants around anger and related hot-spots. Flexibility and agility in seeing both our positions in regards to perspective and our functioning with regards to it, are continually useful characteristics. At the same time, rigidity and the tightening of one's perspectives is a common occurrence in all individuals. Both of these trends exist—simultaneously. It is up to us to feed the one we wish to grow. If we make only a small effort, then the course we follow will be accidental. Who knows where it goes! If we work with intent, with goals in mind, we might step toward those goals.

We seek flexibility. We benefit from the ability to develop novel solutions to challenges faced. We gain wisdom from the cultivation of expanding perspective, and applying all of this to the classroom.

TECHNIQUES:

A portion of the case-stories in this section feature students who have received some form of special education classification—yet the illustrations they present are widely applicable to most classroom settings. The purpose should also be clear. Each action that can help a student feel secure in school, avoid frustration, and appropriately wrestle with strong emotions will mean less school trauma due to anger and its allies.

CREATIVITY (AND VENTURING OUTSIDE THE NORM)

E.G. — DANIEL

A teacher I know solved a large portion of the "unable-to-sit-down" problem by a simple action. Daniel was in third-grade and had difficulty sitting for more than fifteen to thirty minutes at any one time. Being forced to sit in a seat was not going to work. Being allowed to wander continuously around the room was not going to work. Something had to be done with Daniel, and preferably so that he could still benefit from attendance and participation in class.

Karl, the teacher, had a very clever solution. He assigned two seats to Daniel, in the back at opposite corners of the room. Daniel was allowed to travel back and forth at any time—his choice—between his seats. He now had permission to move about whenever he needed to, and was able to stay in the classroom for all subjects and activities.

I know—you may imagine immediate arguments against this solution (two in particular). Creativity, stepping out of the ordinary, can generate considerable resistance at times.

The first argument (from parents or other teachers) centers on the problem of causing distraction for the rest of the class. I've seen many interventions, plans such as this, employed in *inclusion classrooms* (general education classrooms containing one or more students with special needs) where students in the class quickly adjust to the peculiarities and needs of individual students. "Oh, that's just Charlie…" It has warmed my heart to see how fellow students would not only accept the unique needs of these individuals, but support them as well.

The second argument is that other students will want the same treatment, two desks for themselves in this particular situation (see Chapter Six, *Fair versus Equal*). I have found a simple answer to this for students—that works quite well. "You don't need it." This response works because it's true, and the other students know it, even at young ages. I have yet to see a student try to fake the symptoms in order to get what the student-in-need has (though it could be interesting to watch). It just isn't worth it.

There is a third argument to consider in the above action plan: how will it look to school administration? With something like this it's best to work it out with your administration as clearly as possible. Check with them ahead of time on your plan, or have a good sense of their perspective and allowance on issues such as this. If you can show results and clearly sate your logic, you'll have much support on your side. Decide whether to get permission first, or not.

VISUAL SUPPORTS

E.G. — RICKY

Ricky was a fourth-grade boy who loved to ask questions. He loved questions so much that he rarely stopped asking them, repeating himself over and over. This behavior was not productive for him and not fun for anyone else. The staff tried to help him gently change this behavior before he alienated his classmates any more than he already had. Several approaches had failed. There was no change in his behavior. Continually asking questions did not appear to be a behavior he had the ability to control. It was well entrenched.

I had an idea. During the next staff meeting, with seven professionals gathered together, I suggested a plan that I could implement. Yes, was the consensus, let's try it.

When Ricky came to school on Monday I had a talk with him. "Ricky, I have something for you to hold on to that are like tickets, valuable tickets when you choose to spend them. There are ten cards here. Each one has a question mark drawn on it. Here is how they work. Every time you want to ask a question, you simply give a question card to the person you are asking. Then you ask your question.

That means you have ten questions you can ask today. At the end of the day I will hold on to all of the cards, both the ones you spent and the ones you didn't use. When you come back in tomorrow, I will give you ten cards all over again. You will have ten more questions you can ask.

I didn't know if this would work, but if he were to honor the "rules" I had set up (this was very much like a game) then he might limit himself to ten questions a day, which would be a vast improvement. My hope was that this would bring awareness to his behavior, not so much in general terms, but in every moment that he was asking a question, and best if he could notice before he began to ask the question.

The results were stunning. Of course it took a while for him to "get" that each time he was to ask a question he would need a card. The staff would ask, "Is that an important question? Will you give me a card for this?" to remind him of this a few times. He began to remember this well on his own within an hour. It came about that he was so reluctant to let go of any of the cards he held, that he stopped asking all questions, of any kind, ever. We had to talk him into asking the questions that seemed appropriate or necessary, to let him know that some questions are important and useful. He held on to his cards tightly.

About one week later Ricky came to school in the morning and asked for the question cards. I said, "I will not have these cards for you anymore, Ricky." "Why?" he asked. "Because you don't need them anymore." He was silent for a moment, seemingly unsure of what to do. Then he walked away to do something else and said nothing more about it. From that point on he stopped asking questions that were not needed. Except for an occasional, "Is that an important question?" from a teacher, very little was spoken about his prior behavior at all.

Ricky gained many things from this exercise. He made a leap forward in self-awareness in several areas. He was able to see himself asking questions and gained the ability to stop this particular behavior each time before it started, and in a surprisingly short period. He appeared to gain an understanding of the value of question-asking as well, recognizing that questions are tools that can be used to get information or permission. I believe that Ricky also gained insight into his own behavior at a significant level. When the cards were withdrawn, he did not argue—he did not dwell. He moved on. Was this because he didn't understand any of what happened—that it was all simply behavioral modification? Or did he grasp something new about his own behavior? I think here we have a smart boy who was given an opportunity to gain a glimpse into himself, in a gentle (even fun) way, to deal with a repetitive behavior that had a strong grip on him and understand that he no longer needed the props. He had changed, he was freed, and he knew it.

Visual cues can be powerful supports. The cards in this exercise were not only visual but tangible. They struck a chord with Ricky. They also held a strong representation with the target behavior of question-asking. The link was clear—to him and to all. His behavior was instantly highlighted, and he was able to grasp that he could affect his surroundings by directing his own behavior—a significant change over the period of one week.

ANGER TOOLS

STUDENT PARTICIPATION

E.G. — DONNY

Donny, came into an elementary class that a cousin of mine was teaching. Donny had difficulty tolerating other students who came physically too close to him. His way of dealing with it was to strike out and hit them to keep them at bay. Other children soon learned to stay out of the boy's way, but sometimes would forget. Then Bam! It would happen again. The teacher came up with a plan (simple and brilliant it was), one that involved clear boundaries and a strong visual cue, both of which are powerful tools in a situation like this.

Consulting Donny, she put masking-tape on the floor that indicated Donny's private space. Inside the taped square was his space (and he would protect it). Outside the lines was public space. Donny accepted this, and the delineation was clear to him and to all of the other students as well. With delineations being very clear, both defense and avoidance were made simpler, which helped put everyone at ease.

One beautiful result of this was that through the course of the year, Donny was able to reduce the size of the taped square, thus decreasing his private space. He would make the physical change himself, adjusting the tape location. He moved it when he felt he could manage existing in the new space.

In this way he could monitor his own progress and have a direct hand in negotiating it. When the tape was moved, he was the one who moved it, so he had nothing to fight against. He was immediately on board with the change. By the end of the school year he was able to eliminate the tape altogether and get along with his neighbors—a remarkable achievement.

By his participation in the changes, Donny got to experience first-hand how to engage with situations that can be uncomfortable for him. He accepted and even initiated changes that stretched his comfort zone and shrunk the protective zone he had been fiercely protecting. Within a few months Donny was able, on some level, to directly recognize the situation he was caught in, make major changes to that situation, and accept the public into his private space—each of these a major accomplishment for him.

This support for Donny also held a strong visual component, as presented in prior examples. The tape on the floor not only made clear boundaries for all to see, leading to harmony in the classroom—but also allowed for direct, concrete changes leading to a level of freedom for the students of the class, especially the one with most need (Donny). It is easier to defend or to let go of defense of something that is clear and discrete—as opposed to when delineation is gray or undefined. With the latter, much effort and angst goes into establishing the clear boundary, making the resolution of differences more elusive.

The classic approaches listed above for engaging and enlisting student support toward positive change are appropriate for a wide variety of settings. Visual cues in the classroom can be helpful and enlivening for students. Stepping beyond the usual, the ordinary, the status quo—will take courage and may yield interesting results. Part of the courage needed is in not knowing if the results will be as expected, and in addressing pressure from outside. Engaging students in designing and implementing their own educational or behavioral programs is nearly always beneficial, though this approach could take considerable extra time and effort for the teacher.

Balance is key. Finding the right balance between visual stimulation and support and an overly (visually) *busy* classroom; creating a comfortable engagement of student participation in the usually top-down practice of education and behavioral intervention; and assessing the risk/gain potential of novel actions—all must be examined by the teacher before taking action, or the results may be counter-productive.

ANGER TOOLS

BE PREPARED

E.G. — COMPETITOR NUMBER 4

In one instance I was given an awakening shock when applying for a job at a private school for students with special needs. After the interview portion I was asked to actively participate to assist in an adaptive phys-ed class. Each student was assigned an adult to help him/her know when it was his turn to attempt to capture a flag in the center of the room. The boy I supported, about eight years of age, given the number four (each team had a Number 4), ran out and did his best when it was his turn. A bit later Number 4 was called once more and I again gave the prompt that it was his turn. Instead of running out, however, he turned to me at eye level (I was crouching to be at his level) and slapped me hard across the face. Unexpected—to say the least.

So many possible responses loomed with barely seconds to choose. In a firm voice, looking him in the eye and holding my position I said, "Don't *ever* do that again." With further prompt he did run out and do his part. He didn't challenge me again. I chose to express something close to anger, just enough for the situation, and we then got along well. I held no actual anger toward him. This interaction provided a good glimpse into the type of job I would be stepping into.

Yes, by the way, I did get the job and did work there for several years—a never-ending source of opportunity in my effort at not expressing negative emotions (unless intended). I present this anecdote to make it clear that cause for anger can arise at any moment, in any place, and often with no prelude. It's the job of a teacher to be prepared.

PREPARED FOR INTERACTION:

Listed in the following section, "Language," are a number of questions that might help us to *be prepared* for any recurring or novel situations that come our way.

Who knows how I might have reacted to "Competitor Number 4" if I had not had *experience* with this particular list of self-questions and, with considering relevant data and taking quick action.

LANGUAGE:

THE POWER OF LANGUAGE

"Better than a thousand hollow words, is one word that brings peace."
—**Buddha**

Language plays a critical role with every individual—contributing to ease or strain, to success or failure, in our many endeavors. In schools the weight given to language is especially pronounced, both in verbal and written form, as well as through visual and other mediums. The success of each student, the self-image of each student, the effectiveness of each teacher—are all closely linked to the use and understanding of various forms of language (including non-verbal language).

Guiding Principle: When students in a classroom become facile at expressing themselves in words in an atmosphere where communication is welcomed, resorting to *striking out at others* diminishes and the incidence of anger decreases. We begin our discussion of language aspects relating to classroom anger, with communication as a foremost purpose of language.

COMMUNICATION:

Communication is a huge topic, spanning myriad forms, purposes, and degrees of subtlety. It is included here to emphasize its importance to students and teachers in the academic, social, and personal-growth worlds of schooling. Poor communication skills can lead to frustration, being teased or bullied, and poor grade scores for students. Inadequate communication skills can lead to considerable blockage, such as brilliant scientists being unable to get their valuable information across to others. It happens all the time. Ability is wasted, information is stuck, answers are missed.

For students, any of the unwanted results of insufficient communication skills can lead to a frustration that often grows into anger and results in the need for teacher intervention. In addition, students might gain only a small portion of what is possible for them during their school careers—a lose-lose situation.

Communication skills include language such as:
- Expressive—speaking, singing, lecturing, debating...
- Receptive—listening, attending in conversation, sensing...
- Non-verbal—recognizing body language and facial expression in others
- Non-standard—idioms, colloquialisms, inference ...

Dr. Carey J. Green speaks of the importance of communication skills in his book, *Success Skills for School and Career*.(2) He identifies the two primary steps in communication as: good *listening skills* and effective *articulation*—being able to communicate well with others by getting to the point and being understood. Carey goes on to express how the same academic and general skills needed for school success will later translate into *soft skills* when out of school and "life is coming at you"—soft skills such as time management, work ethic, critical thinking, communication skills, and being able to read and synthesize that information for use.

The smartest student might fail in school if she does not have good communication skills. A problem might be that tests and other assessments administered measure test-taking ability more than intelligence or knowledge. This is a very common occurrence for students, especially students who do not fit within the norm for processing speed, favored communication avenues, academic and pre-academic exposure, or cultural familiarity. Only a narrow range of ability will be adequately assessed, though the tests are usually far more widely applied in representing *student ability levels*.

Some of the most common sources of anger for students in schools are from feeling inadequate, getting poor grades, and being ostracized by others. Each of these difficulties may be lessened by good communication skills. The problem for many schools is that such skills are taught only incidentally or indirectly. Specific programs targeting communication skills could make a significant difference not only for students who show a specific need for it, but for all students.

NON-VERBAL LANGUAGE:

Much is said between individuals without a word being spoken. This is essentially a form of continuous messaging. There is always something to see in a person's look, posture, proximity, expression, eyes, and more if we are able or interested in noticing. This silent world of communication can be rich and interesting, or frustrating as hell, depending on your perceptive/interpretive abilities. Some individuals with specific challenges are particularly prone to difficulty here, as you will see in Chapter Six—Classified.

E.G. — JENNA

Jenna was a student in a small private school. She was scheduled for annual testing, and arrangements were made for this to occur. Against the current teacher's recommendation, it was suggested that she visit her home-district school for the testing to be done. The home school district insisted. On the day of testing Jenna was brought to the district school, which was only minimally familiar to her.

We soon received a call that the school had gone on lockdown and that Jenna was missing. It didn't take long for trouble to brew.

She had walked out of the testing office, angry. She then walked out of the building as well. When she could not be immediately found, the lockdown procedure was engaged. She had been there for only one half-hour.

When asked later what the issue was, Jenna replied (referring to the testing professional), "She talked to me like I was stupid." It had infuriated her. I hear this as a common complaint. The attitude, nuance, and language of the professional created an immediate barrier—and worse, no viable teacher-student learning/rapport was possible. This kind of disconnect by the professional would mean that any testing and evaluation would be erroneous, invalid, and misleading—and it could lead to worse, as we have seen in this instance.

Jenna was quickly found in the schoolyard that morning. This situation was smoothly resolved, but sometimes these incidents don't end well. I've often seen such problematic situations devolve into chaos. Jenna ended up being tested in the school she attended, where we were familiar with her and how best to work with her. If Jenna had managed to stay for the testing in her home-district school and survived the testing professional that did not understand her or how to communicate with her, then the evaluation would have been considered complete. The results would have been deemed accurate and valid and used in the preparation of programming for her, likely built upon false or incomplete information—a weak foundation.

STRAIGHT-TALK:

Honest statements, simply delivered, can often be heard quickly and clearly.

E.G. — LEE

We were hiking a portion of the Appalachian Trail as a class activity one beautiful autumn day. Lee, then ten years old, stopped on the trail and waited for me to pass. When I reached him he began to complain, "I can't believe how far he is making us hike," speaking of the other teacher ahead. "This is so boring," he said with great passion.

"Would you rather be sitting in the classroom?" I asked. (He found no sympathy here). He was silent.

After running up and down the trail for a while more, Lee ran back to me to ask, "Why is everybody so slow?"— again with a complaining voice. He was moving toward anger. I smiled inwardly at his contradictory complaints.

"Lee," I said. "When you are running along the trail, enjoying that movement, it is *your body and your heart talking*. You are having fun, and it's a fine thing to see. You are very graceful.

When you are complaining and feeling bored, that's *your head talking*. Right now listen to your body and heart. Ignore those complaining thoughts. Your head will be there when you need it. You don't need it now."

He said nothing, and ran off down the trail—like an animal in the woods—which he was.

ART FORMS: (MUSIC, DANCE, FINE ART, ARCHITECTURE, POETRY, AMBIENCE ART…)

Those who participate in any way in the many forms of art can experience strong communication—whether creator, purveyor, receiver, or witness. Though art is often considered a tangential form of communication, at most, upon close observance there is much to be seen in the depth and breadth of communication through art. Some communication may even persist over the passage of centuries.

ASKING QUESTIONS:

The asking of a question can communicate much to a person. Attitude, stance, and action needed can be transmitted, for example, without any direct reference included. The act alone of asking might have a strong effect on someone and open up possibilities that might not arise otherwise.

ANGER TOOLS

E.G. — BRIAN

I recall one time having to consider my approach to a co-teacher, Brian, regarding a sensitive situation. It had followed a meeting between a parent with her son and me, into which Brian had inserted himself. I became concerned as Brian's emotions pushed him close to words that would be difficult to pull back from once spoken. I knew that certain things said in the presence of mother and son could have unwanted effects for this student, and might even necessitate other actions to be taken—official ones, whether I thought them useful or harmful.

When, later in the day, I had the opportunity to speak with Brian, I had to carefully review my options as I considered my reactions to what appeared as inappropriate behavior on his part and the ease with which I could have let anger speak on my part. He had been able to keep only a dangerously loose control on his speaking, and hadn't even been invited to the conference. He just saw it taking place and decided to sit in.

As it turned out, the effort to avoid accusation in my words and tone made it possible for a useful dialogue to take place. I observed a choice, and instead of going with my first inclination, "Why did you say such negative things about Jayson to his mother at the meeting this morning? It was dangerous and inappropriate..." I used a considered approach of "How do you feel the parent meeting went this morning?" leaving it wide open.

This choice allowed room for greater reflection on his part. The result was a great deal of self-reflection. "Terrible," Brian replied, then proceeded to be forthcoming and truthful about how he felt and acted. Some of his observations were insightful and would hopefully inform his choices going forward.

I could easily have framed the question I asked from my own emotional standpoint, leaving limited room for an open answer in return. A more reactive response to this type of approach is likely. I worded my question without judgment, allowing an honest, self-searching effort in return. Yet, there was more to it than this. Not only were my words clean (without blame) but my inner stance was as well. I had had to adjust my inner judgement so as to not transmit negativity. Consequently, we were able to address the current situation rather than dance around a reaction to an opinion or accusation coming from me. We then set about developing a plan of action for the development of this teacher, Brian, when dealing with strong emotions. We both gained from this situation.

Questions are used in many intentional ways, such as with psychoanalysis, marketing, or interrogation. Questions may be innocent or wily, shallow or deep—or used for self-exploration as championed by Sophocles—*Know Thyself.*

E.G. — REFLECT, RESPOND, REACT

Working with college graduate students, I often questioned the difference between the terms *reflect, respond, react*. Graduate students frequently encounter these terms in assignments or quizzes. It often proves difficult for them to adequately describe or understand the differences in these terms. So, depending on the trajectory of the ensuing discussion, I might ask other questions or give cues to help stimulate the direction of their thinking, such as: consider the speed of each or what might be the difference in the quality of results of each of these actions? The questions were not delivered as a search for information from the students as much as a way to deepen their ability to self-search and make necessary links between topics. The questions were internal way-finders for the students.

Voluminous written material is available on the art of asking questions. Different perspectives and techniques are within easy reach—at least for the reading. What I do with the information depends on what I might garner from it. Why should I, as a teacher, not put at least as much effort into asking a question as I put into writing test questions for my students? And if any teacher has ever done this casually, he will note immediate, unwelcome consequences. Care is needed to do this well. There are a couple of points to be made here.

I wish to emphasize the importance of intentional questioning—of carefully crafting a question so that it might enliven or calm a classroom as appropriate to the moment, so that a volatile situation with a student might be circumvented or a favorable solution for a student in need can be explored.

For example, in the book *Getting to Calm*, Kastiner and Wyatt focus much attention on framing questions and conversation with teens and tweens so that desired results can be obtained.(3) Desired results might mean: encouraging self-reflection on the part of the young adult without setting off defensive reactions, solidifying communication between adult and teen, or re-establishing parental authority in an acceptable manner. An example of this can be found in a suggested phrasing offered in the Kastiner and Wyatt book, "What threw you off course?" With this simple question several things are established.

- This was not a typical behavior for the teen. It was an "off-course" behavior—recognizing the teen's usually good behavior.
- There is a sense that the teen can get himself back "on course."
- There is a request for an explanation—reinforcing the parental role that the teen must still answer to.
- There is an invitation to have an adult discussion about a particular incident and about behavior in general.

With this question a balance is struck between a firmness and a yielding, acceptance, and challenge—recognizing a need for balance with independence and responsibility in the young adult.

LANGUAGE AND THE TEACHER

Language can be dangerous. Words spoken carelessly can lead us into pitfalls that are difficult to climb out of. Language can be used to push fear, suspicion and hatred, as is too often done with intent. Language can be a strong *tool for good* as well—or simply a beautiful medium. Words carry a power within and around a classroom. Language is a fundamental tool in the effort to prepare students and teachers to address anger in a healthy way, and to provide learning on valuable self-monitoring techniques.

VOICE:

Voice is a major component of language and communication. It is a good place to begin self-monitoring efforts for a teacher.

E.G. — LISA

When I first started working at a school with students who often presented a particular management challenge, I recognized a need for language control. Every time Lisa, my co-teacher (the experienced one) left the room, the noise level quickly rose. When she returned, the noise level dropped almost immediately. It seemed like magic. "I need to know how to do that," I said. And there I began an unending process of refining and refreshing what I know and what I learn about teaching in a classroom.

I began to watch how Lisa spoke, how she changed inflection, volume, or the sharp or soft qualities of her voice. I noticed when she stepped into a situation to speak (even before I perceived a problem brewing) to prevent any escalation of trouble. I noticed when she chose words that left latitude for the student and when she spoke in words that set sharp boundaries. I started to more closely notice these same areas of voice and language in myself as well. Learning came quickly then, and much of it was self-driven.

WHAT LANGUAGE DO YOU SPEAK?:

Sometimes I speak "Aloof." Sometimes I speak "Impatience." Sometimes "Respect," "Fear," "Confidence," or "Joy." Sometimes I speak

"Uninterested." This is the language behind the dialogue that I use. This is the language, the message, that is heard often more loudly than the words that are spoken.

The effort to notice and to affect the way I communicate can be more difficult on some days than on others. I know that on the days when I experience lower energy, I'm at risk of losing connection with students, or of dropping into casual or careless communication. The language behind words can speak boredom, irritation, or the wish to be anywhere else. It can also be, "I am interested," or at the least, "I will listen, fully."

As one practices over years, the ability to notice inner voice and inner stance will come with greater ease in the course of each school day. The ability for us to notice and to influence our inner voice will become more fluid and effective, leading to increased control of oneself as well as the classroom atmosphere. At the same time there are thresholds over which we will not advance, forms of deeper communication, unless intent and effort are repeatedly applied.

The questions we ask of ourselves will influence this learning, such as: what does my current inner voice usually say to me, and have I any real control in this—or, how do my personal preferences and comfort levels guide or limit my thinking and my behavior?

EXERCISE 11:
Words That Whisper in My Ear

> Look for the words that speak to you from inside, as you step into teaching moments or interactions with children and young adults. What are the thoughts, attitudes, and phrases that repeat themselves? Evidence of these might be noticeable in your facial expression, body stance, or openness to listening. Watch yourself over a period of three weeks, making an effort to catch moments of inner speaking every day.
>
> In the beginning, success with this effort will likely be elusive. You might notice self-talk here and there, yet miss most of it (99%?) because people generally have a constant tape-loop

going that has the effect of numbing attention. Thoughts run and run and run. (Some counter efforts to this busy mental state may be found in Chapter Seven—The Inner Approach.)

It would help to practice this exercise in situations outside of school, as well as in. Mental chatter may be found in any situation. Try to not judge any of what is observed. Simply note. Later, if you wish to effect change, attempts can be made.

SELF-TALK:

We spoke in the prior section about the voices and attitudes that are continually speaking to us, whether we invite them to or not.

I might hold an inner position of, "The teacher is always right," or "I will always engage with what the student has to say." Though quite different in their manifestation and effect, both of these positions can stifle flexibility in any teacher who holds them tightly—and this is exactly what we often do, without our awareness of doing so. If I was to embrace an attitude of "I can't handle any confrontation right now" as I interact with a student, I am immediately limited in my ability to hear what is being said, appreciate the other's point of view, or take appropriate action.

The tone of voice and the words I select (or unintentionally use), will be guided by any preset emotions, perspectives, and beliefs that I carry. If my mind is already set and the script already written (or even simply outlined) then my effectiveness plummets—for I can only hope that the position I bring to a situation is solely the one that is needed. But what are the odds of that?

Another side to this condition is *intentional self-talk*.

Two approaches are needed for this effort—

- This first essential step is to cultivate a perspective of self-observation and awareness as has been referred to repeatedly in these pages. Practice this until it becomes commonplace for you, an easy and regular activity.
- The next step is to prepare one's thinking and language ahead

ANGER TOOLS

of time, before applying it to classroom situations. We prepare through *practice* and *principle*.

PRACTICE:

Since I can't review individually all there is to consider when speaking with students at the moment I'm speaking, I will practice ahead of time. I'll watch each conversation I have each time I speak, pulling from this a list of things to consider, and I'll consider as many of the items on the list as I am able. I might then ask as I engage, "Are any of the considerations relevant now as I speak or listen?" "Can I *do* anything about their presence to set aside or to engage these considerations?" "Is this within my ability?"

The answers will come with the effort to observe—to observe impartially, without preference for what is comfortable or for what mirrors my beliefs. I've found it helpful, as well, to write down a sample list for myself (as presented below) to help each question rise into consciousness where I can deliberately study it. As it is, everyone considers various options and consequences when speaking— though to widely varying degrees and without consistent monitoring of appropriateness.

The goal then is to be able to bring all that I've learned by these efforts into each interaction—in a flash. I won't need to go down the list deliberating on each one (like Terminator 1 did in the motel room when approached by the Janitor) since the list will have become a part of me, of my understanding. I'll be free to interact and to move in the direction I see as best with many of the following considerations guiding me—silently.

A sample list of considerations:
- Do I need to speak at all?
- Do I know what I am talking about?
- Is there spinach on my teeth?
- Does it *matter* if there is spinach on my teeth?
- Am I sounding shrill?
- Am I being patronizing or aloof?

- How can this interaction empower or weaken me?
- Am I coming to this with an open or cloudy mind?
- Is there emotional baggage that can interfere here?
- What does this person want from me?
- Can I keep my attention right here and nowhere else?
- Is my approach charged or neutral, alert or sleepy, relaxed or tight, direct or circuitous, assertive, aggressive or timid?
- Shall I bring humor in or low stress discussion—and do I have the energy to act in this way?
- Do I believe that a six-year-old can take a self-reflective position?

As a teacher there may be other, more specific, considerations as well:
- What does this student need right now?
- What does the class need right now?
- Can these two blend?
- How hard or sharp does my tone need to be?
- Might this student benefit best from a shock like strong discipline (e.g., suspension)?
- Do I need to bring other parties into this conversation?
- What would be good next steps?
- Am I being defensive?
- Is this student aware that I am on her side?
- What parameters must I work within?

MORE PRACTICE:

- Straight-talk—Be truthful and to the point. *Soften the blow* only as much as necessary. Be direct (see earlier in this Chapter).
- Presence—Hold a sense that you are available to this person. ("I will listen, I will help if I am able.")
- Respect—Speak as though the student is mature for her age/grade. Set high expectations for her, then watch with objectivity. Don't underestimate her capacity to understand and appreciate subtleties and interconnections or to sit with a bit of

ANGER TOOLS

mystery. Yet, be ready to supply some of these connections where appropriate.

PRINCIPLE:

What ideals and practices do you hold dear? These are the underlying feelings and beliefs that influence every move you make and color every thought you have. These will affect the language that you use and the way you communicate with students. We have spoken in several sections of this book about the effort to uncover the hidden beliefs that each of us holds. I refer specifically here to principles that we consciously hold, to a light or strong degree, beyond and including the classroom.

For example, where do you range along the spectrum of—at one end: "A unique individual stands in front of me, I am interested,"—and at the other end: "Children should be seen and not heard." We might even recognize moments when we are drawn toward one direction, such as the latter position above, while consciously pushing ourselves in the opposite direction. We attempt to move from one position toward the other since it is a goal of ours to experience and act in a chosen way. This shows great strength. And it is strength that is needed, along with our energy and ability level on any given day, that will determine our level of success in going against tendencies ingrained in us.

Sometimes it helps to keep specific ideals that resonate with you as reminders, in the forefront of your attention. This is why people are drawn toward aphorisms, though the real strength lies in learning how to keep the meaning alive in us. A sampling follows. May they carry more weight than simply words.

- *Keep your word.*
- *Always leave a place better than you found it.*
- *Finish what you begin.*
- *Respect personal religious and spiritual choices.*
- *By teaching others I myself will learn.*
- and perhaps the most universal—the Golden Rule:
    - *Do unto others what you would have them do unto you.*

With time the efforts presented in this section on teacher language will become more "internalized" in us. We won't need to consciously bring them to mind as often to feel their influence. They'll become an automatic guide for us, steering us in directions that we've chosen to develop. The thought processes that we develop will begin to inform our feelings as well, which will quickly be present in any future interaction—making us better able to "Be Prepared."

PLAY:

When language and play go hand-in-hand, they bring a quality to interactions that can counter negativity before, during, and after difficult moments. Reading, speaking, and listening-language fun can offer benefits for child intellectual and emotional growth, bonding between individuals, and a smoothly running classroom. And language-play can be just plain fun. Too often school teachers and administrators are so pressed to produce specific results that there seems to be no time for the natural rhythm of play or rest. The serious endeavor loses its place in the classroom balance and becomes a somber weight. All learning progress is diminished when it feels too heavily pushed on students.

In a survey that reached more than 81,000 students in 110 high schools across 26 states, Indiana University's High School Survey of Student Engagement (HSSSE) found that "two out of three high-school students in a large survey say they are bored in class every day... About 30 percent of the students indicate they are bored due to lack of interaction with teachers...The same reasons for boredom could explain high drop-out rates" as well, the article goes on to say. (4)

Boredom can grate on students (or anyone)—kind of like sitting at a desk made of sandpaper. Who would want do endure this? Yet simple alternatives exist.

Consider the quality that language-play could bring into classrooms, where the play is appropriate to the maturity level and students become engaged. Even to simply keep a sense of playfulness at the ready can make the school day so much more enjoyable for student and teacher alike. Some factors in the game of play:

- Don't undervalue the simple game of "hangman." One student I worked with was essentially non-verbal yet brilliant. When I first met her she would look away whenever I called on her or even looked in her direction. Eventually she was brave enough to come to the board, after seeing the rest of her class and myself having fun, to challenge the class with a hangman word of her choice. Neither I, nor anyone else in the classroom (including two other teachers) could determine the full meaning of the word, even after seeing it—though it makes perfect sense to me now. See if you can get it. Fourteen letters: caligynephobia. (Spell-check does not recognize this word.) Combine the meaning of the three parts of the word. Explore words of similar spelling, prefix, or base to zero in on a meaning— (California, calligraphy, etc.).

- Playing word games not only promotes learning, but also can create an atmosphere where the joy of learning is recognized and a statement is made that it is okay to have fun in class. Many class-wide games are now available for teachers to adapt to the classroom such as "Kahoot." We've had many hours of both fun and learning with this app in a high school setting. Students were eager to take quizzes and to challenge one another with this program, at all ability levels. The teachers created the questions, and would set up teams where it seemed appropriate. I was impressed with the students' response to this form of learning and testing.

WORD-PLAY AND PUNS—A SAMPLING:

- Max, at seven years old, hearing his mother say, "This is spectacular," while climbing several sets of stairs to a condo deep within the Colorado Rockies says, "No mom, this is steptacular."
- One time, when several of us were hiking, we came across some scat on a wooden walk-bridge. After careful inspection we deduced that it might be from a mink. Later, on the return trip, Asher (seven years old) said, "Watch out where you step or you will be a minkenpoop."
- One evening we were about to hold hands at the start of the

evening meal, as is often done. Ezra did not want to join on this night. I said something to him like "It won't hurt," to which his older, eight-year-old brother smiled and said, "Pain-a-petit."

- Trying to motivate my grandsons for a family outing (sometimes they will go against whatever is suggested by adults) I made a game of it. I offered only the first three letters of our destination. I said, "Give your brother this clue: *s-c-r*." And by the way, you'll love it," I said, "—you always do."

The younger immediately said, "Bouldering." He was correct. He caught the "always love it" part, but I did not tell him that yet. He had to carry the clue to his brother. The younger came back downstairs from delivering the clue and said, "He said 'Scram.'"

I laughed. I later asked the older if the "scram" was to tell his little brother to leave, or to name the activity (We were to go "scrambling" on the rocks). "Both," he said, as I had guessed.

- Stephen, a professional musician, had a mountain-biking run-in between a small tree and his left small finger. The finger had suffered trauma (the tree was unfazed) and could not function with strength. All the fingers of his left hand were needed for playing guitar, so some repair needed to be done. After minor surgery he told me that if the injury had been to the right hand, he would have left it alone. "So," I said, "if it was your right hand, you would have left it— but since it was your left hand, you had to right it. Yes?" He smiled.

- Preparing grandsons with word-play: As everyone was getting ready to sit at the dinner table one evening, I reminded Ezra (aged five) to wash his hands. This is not something he generally runs to do. Tonight, after I reminded him a couple of times, he shuffled his feet a few inches at a time toward the bathroom. "Grandpa, I am making progress. See, Grandpa?" he announced occasionally. It would have taken likely four hours to get to the wash room at that speed. He had a smile on his face as he chewed on a strip of turkey bacon.

ANGER TOOLS

PREFIX/BASE/SUFFIX EXPLORATION:
(SUFFIX OR BASE WORDS WILL WORK AS WELL)

- Often I jump away from a lesson I am presenting to play with prefixes—*mort*, for example.

Students come up with (or not) mortuary, mortician, mortifying, morbid (slightly different), mortal. By now they have the meaning, and occasionally someone mentions mortgage (especially if I make this jump when teaching about interest and mortgage rates). By the way, where do you think the connection is with the meaning of mort in the word mortgage? And I might add in: Morticia (*The Adams Family*), Mordor (*Lord of the Rings*), Mordred (Arthurian legend), Voldimort (*Harry Potter*), or various Spanish language links.

We might also look at a prefix or word part like "dur" (durable, endure, duration, Dura-cell, etc.), or list all of the prefixes in our language that mean "not." This is play, and we do have fun. Oh, and did anyone mention learning?

Simply, play in the classroom can engage students, promote valuable mental connections, and help minimize the difficulties of stress and anger.

ANGER AS A USEFUL TOOL:

In the exploration of anger it will be found that there are individuals who welcome anger as part of their lives, others who might complain about its presence but are in no way willing to let it go, those who fear it, and those who have learned to find freedom from its grip. Of these various individuals there are those who will state that it serves a useful purpose for them.

Can anger actually be a useful thing, something to intentionally bring forth—or to let rip? Clearly different opinions and perspectives will be encountered, including from those individuals who may be seriously fooling themselves. I begin the discussion here with a few personal observations:

- The usefulness of anger can be considered a relative matter (related to specific goals).
- Anger can be used in certain settings—under certain conditions—in a useful way.
- Anger is rarely employed in a useful manner.
- Those who say that they can use anger without being used by it, most often are wrong.
- The presence of anger can be a good pointer toward a problem that needs attention.
- An ultimate goal here is to function outside the grip of anger—to be free, unhooked.

ANGER IS NOT A **CLEAN** TOOL

E.G. — TED

In 1941, on the morning of the last day of the regular baseball season, Ted Williams had a batting average of .3996. His coach suggested that he play it safe and sit out the double-header on the last day so that his average would jump to .400 (and as anyone who follows baseball knows, even a .300 average in the major league is a huge accomplishment, and anything even close to a .400 is a rarity). Williams would have none of it. He wanted to earn it or miss it, not average up to it.

In the two games that day he came to the plate eight times. Four hits (not a small feat) would have locked it in for him—less than that number and he would miss the .400 mark. He went on to hit safely in six out of eight at-bats, and ended with an average of .406. No baseball player has reached a season average of .400 since, or even come close, more than seventy-five years later.

Ted Williams was also a combat pilot in the Korean War, flying in thirty-nine combat missions. On one of those flights his plane was hit by enemy fire. He was able to fly the badly damaged plane all the way back to base, crash-landing at 225 mph, sliding for a mile. The plane then exploded in flames seconds after he had escaped. He kicked what was left of the plane once he got out. When asked how he made it back he replied, "I fly better mad."

He also used anger in the game of baseball—anger at the pitcher, at sports-writers, and at himself. It fueled him and helped his focus. But there was a downside to this as well. For example, when he struck out one time, he angrily threw his bat. It flew into the stands, striking a fan and sending her to the hospital. He said he was mad at himself after getting strike three. The anger that started as a motivator and positive support turned into a dangerous influence when unchecked.

THE EXPRESSION OF ANGER IN THE CLASSROOM

So the question arises: is there any legitimate place for anger in the classroom? Under certain conditions the intentional expression of anger can be a useful tool. Yet, in a classroom setting or any other high-stakes situation, great care must be observed. The first and foremost condition I would place on the expression of anger in any classroom, is *"Do not express anger when angry!"* This is perhaps the most important point to be made about the classroom use of anger. We explore.

Anger expression can be very effective at getting the attention of a student or class, at making a point, or stopping a dangerous action. Anger might be expressed through a look, a word, a clap of the hands. Intentionally used, with appropriate parameters, anger can be quite effective. I've been in situations where a dangerous moment could best be averted with a sharp, loud "Stop!" (as in the story *Marie* below) I've seen students cut off a certain train of behavior when they felt they were approaching a teacher's "red-line" of anger. There are moments when anger is what the student can hear best.

But there is danger here, danger in teaching the student to depend on the teacher's red-line rather than developing increased self-control. There is the danger that a teacher might misread a situation and use anger at an inappropriate time, creating far more difficulties than solutions. There is danger that students might try to bring out the anger in a teacher, to see if they can succeed in pushing the right buttons. And a classic difficulty, for teachers and anyone else, is that she might come under the spell of the anger—no longer in control, but *thinking* that she is still in charge.

The intentional expression of anger is best done with our own awareness of positive feelings for the student. This is not the usual state of things, for when anger arises, care for the target party evaporates immediately. Yet, I suggest that when expressing anger, it's important to always keep a sense of helping and caring, in heart and in mind, for each student. Holding caring isn't easy, and the expression of anger may be a tool that is best left aside by most teachers, never to be used in the classroom.

Consider this. At the moment of expressing anger, can you choose to smile if you wish, truly smile—smile at the situation, at yourself? Can you smile with caring toward the person you are engaged with? Can you stop with ease, or in spite of internal forces shouting at you to launch into the anger? If you can stop and experience caring for the other, then you are in a position to safely express anger, briefly and carefully. But you must be able to easily set it aside—or you have been fooling yourself. This is a most difficult task, yet possible.

E.G. — MARIE

> While directing a middle-school program, I was helping a student with a project—when I heard loud sounds coming from outside the room. Suddenly, a student came running into the room and was followed by a loud kick to the door by a second student, with enough force to have sent a football through the goalposts from fifty yards away. Marie was chasing Paul with a serious intent. As the door slammed open I yelled, "Stop!" with a fierce, angry voice. All action from everyone stopped

immediately. I then stepped into the melee and retained just enough anger in my voice to keep the participants carefully listening to me. A potentially dangerous or destructive moment was rapidly diffused. The entire situation ended quickly, and individuals walked away. I let the anger-voice go. No residue.

ANGER AS A TOOL

Two Examples:

E.G. — TERRY

Terry would not put his cell phone away in the classroom. During a break the teacher in the room came to tell me about the problem and asked me to address it. Terry, I was told, wouldn't put it away when asked to do so. I needed to better understand what was occurring. As I went into the room and said, "Terry, please come to the office". I received a question in reply: "Why do I need to go with you?"

This could have been an innocent question, but that's not what I heard in his voice. It was more a voice of defiance, a measure of challenge. Many students were still in the classroom at that time, and I had to decide on how public to make my comments. I saw that giving him an explanation at that moment would give him too much power. I didn't engage (often teachers should not).

"You don't need to know why – just come," I said with a strong voice and walked out of the room, expecting him to follow. By this statement and the touch of anger in my voice, I established two primary things. First, that I was the one who held the power, and second, yes indeed—he did have some behavior to answer for. I also walked out ahead of him so that he could set his pace at walking out of the room without being lorded over by the teacher, and he would also lose a good opportunity for a passive-aggressive response such as moving very slowly.

At the same time I had initiated a challenge. If he had chosen not to follow me out of the room (a possibility we must all be ready for) that would have escalated the confrontation. I was aware of this, and it is one of the reasons that I take caution in such a public action. I had to be willing to go the distance with him, to continue to maintain the teacher power-position. I would have dropped everything else to stay with this situation to its conclusion. If I didn't, then I would lose a great deal of disciplinary strength with the entire class.

As it was, Terry did follow, quietly. In the office I asked, "Tell me what's going on." He admitted to having his cell phone out, and explained why. His reasoning was not bad. It could have affected his ability to keep his job.

"Do you understand the position you put the teacher in when you don't communicate this clearly and try to work out a solution—when you directly ignore a directive or break a rule that's clearly in place?" He did. From there I asked, "How shall we handle this?" We went on to work out a solution.

The reason I had given the angry reaction to him wasn't because he was bad, or because he was disrespectful, or because I was angry. It was tactical. He had challenged my authority at that moment as a teacher of that classroom, even though I was not the teacher in the class at that time of the cell-phone problem. I had to be sure the authority stayed with me. A better solution would have been for the other teacher, the one that was originally teaching, to take care of the problem—but that didn't turn out to be possible. The teacher and I would speak later.

There are situations where the smallest use of well-placed anger can go a long way. But the anger would be considered small only if the user, myself in this case, is able to quickly let it go. (It's also important to have a sense of how the student will handle the anger expressed.) In the office I held a firm stance while at the same time a genuine caring for the student. Terry knew this. Rather than weakening our relationship, the interaction strengthened it. He knew that I was on his side. He knew also that the anger was not inappropriate. In the classroom he had broken rules and was rude to the teacher—so he accepted what I sent his way.

EXERCISE 12:
The Anger Goal

> Determine a situation where the use of anger might be useful and appropriate if you can. If you cannot, don't worry. Wait until the moment arises—though it might never do so. Fine.
>
> As you engage, notice how it feels inside. Are you able to keep a clean separation from the anger, expressing it while not being bullied by it? Notice the outer results of your use of anger. Are these results what you were hoping for? Would you call it successful? Were there unexpected consequences, and are these within a range of acceptable? Study this effort. Determine how to do it best, or if it is even worth engaging in at all.
>
> What might be helpful is to create a set of criteria (up to five items) before actual practice—for how you will gauge whether the effort went the way you wished. How did the actuality compare to the predetermination you had established? This will make it easier to answer all of the questions in the paragraph above.

Sometimes the use of anger can be a simple and effective tool—

E.G. — THE RABBI

I once invited a Rabbi to speak to a private school I managed (we rented space from the Jewish Community Center), and to answer questions from the students and teachers. Within his talk he told a parable of a *Rabbi and a delivery man*.

The person who was to deliver goods to the Jewish

community from the ship that brought them to shore refused to move. He sat upon his horse, his wagon all loaded with materials belonging to the good people who could not get him to budge. The delivery man was insisting on more money, beyond the agreed-upon amount, claiming that extra time had been needed. The villagers scolded and wept and reasoned with the man—to no avail. Then along came the Rabbi, slow and steady.

"Ahh, now he can reason with this man and get him to move," they thought.

The Rabbi walked quietly up to the man sitting upon his horse, and proceeded to lambast and threaten him in such a loud voice that it made the jaws of the villagers drop. They were shocked! Never had they heard the Rabbi speak this way, nor seen a whip in his hand as it was today.

They were shocked, as well, to see the delivery man quickly begin doing his assigned task to deliver the goods.

"Why did you speak to the man that way?" they asked.

"Because sometimes this is the only voice a man can hear."

The Rabbi then slowly and calmly turned his back and walked away.

USING FOUND ANGER

Some angry moments that arise can be useful in select settings. A teacher who is prepared to take advantage of these moments will create a positive learning opportunity.

E.G. — BRONX DANCE

It was late Saturday afternoon in the Bronx, and I was teaching dance to a group of students. The students were at this weekend class in order to make up a gym credit they'd missed in school. The program also focused on personal development and professional development, all of which turned out to be of great value to the students.

The form of dance, called *Movements*, was developed by G. I. Gurdjieff and Thomas de Hartmann (5)—with influence from ancient traditions from around the globe—and designed to develop the power of attention and knowledge in the dancers. Among other strong components of the dance is cooperation and silent communication among the dancers—aiming toward developing group presence.

This proved to be fertile ground for discussion as I led these young adults through some of the simpler group movements. Anger was popping up all through the group. "He did this." "She didn't do that." We used these complaints as starting points for discussions about anger, about expectation, about communication, about our reactionary selves, about being part of a group, about caring for one-another, about whether there was even value in having these very discussions, and more. The personal learning was rich. And as we continued to practice on following Saturdays it was evident that, though things were not perfect, individuals were coalescing as a group. This was not simply because they had practiced the dances. I could also see a growing sense of support for (rather than a blaming of) one another and a genuine effort at building something cohesive.

ANGER AS INDICATOR

We may find indicators of anger (found anger) anytime and anywhere. Twenty-seven indicators are listed in the first Chapter in this book, under *Manifestations of Anger*. We might focus in on any item on this list to look deeper into how it relates to anger and to ourselves in particular. Take, for example, number seven, "I bristle at teacher evals or any bit of criticism". What does it tell us that we are defensive in such matters, that we react strongly to criticism or take any critique as criticism? What is it that is hurt in us?

We might study whether our feelings are appropriate to the level of the situation or if we are even accurate in interpretation of events.

We might investigate whether we react similarly in different situations and whether we behave with automatic reaction or measured response? We might note whether we are inclined toward criticism of others. The choice is ours. The results of our efforts may vary widely, from deeply useful to useless, depending on our willingness and ability.

Working with someone who could act as a guide might help with this as well. We might begin to see patterns in our feeling and behavior, to anticipate what will follow. What is then created is the opportunity to change the direction we are going in if we so wish. We learn to read the danger signs arising for us. We might then usefully place our attention and our action.

CLASS-WIDE ANGER TOPICS:

Having class discussion around the topic of anger can create opportunities for students to learn about themselves in relation to anger, glean methods of grappling with anger, and perhaps find ways to sidestep or let go of anger. Insights might also center on triggers and signs leading up to anger. Teachers can benefit both by observing what the class thinks and needs, and by teacher self-study.

Discussing deep topics such as this might also bring students together as a group, even when they are not all in agreement regarding what is discussed. Don't be surprised to notice the level of maturity of these individuals rising as well, as they learn to discuss difficult inner questions and conditions—aspects of the *inner landscape*.

A sampling of topics and questions that might arise:
- How do you feel when anger is aimed at you?
- Does anger ever feel okay or appropriate?
- How about when *you* are angry—is that okay?
- How long does it take you to get over an angry moment?
- Can you tell when you are leading up to an angry outburst?

- Could you stop it from happening if you wished to do so? Do you have specific techniques?

Invite students to come up with topics, or start with one question and see where the conversation travels.

DEEPER USE OF ANGER

Anger is everywhere. And for that reason, along with its powerful influence on us, it is a perfect medium for efforts at self-development. Anyone who wishes to explore how they themselves operate—how they think, feel, act, interact, or react—will have ample opportunity to do so with this topic. What next arises is the possibility of using the discovered knowledge and understanding to more firmly stand our ground when faced with such strong emotions, and to apply these strengths in many other settings. We widen our learning, look deeper into our own functioning, and hopefully develop a measure of freedom.

As we wrestle these bits of freedom from the clutches of anger, bitterness, and self-rightcousness, we strengthen our ability to do the same in other areas of our being. We learn how to find strength in ourselves. We learn how we operate as a well-functioning human being, and how we might have a hand in further developing that functioning. Anger is an opportune area for us to focus efforts on, as we not only reduce its control over us, but extrapolate the new knowledge to other facets of ourselves.

[Please see Chapter Nine (e.g.—*Vermont Holiday*) for an example of this.]

EXERCISE 13:
Observing Effective Anger

> Watch for anger around you. Watch for it in the world of politics, education, marriage—or wherever it shows up. Note whether the anger displayed has any useful qualities to it, any useful benefits that you can see. (This can be difficult to actually notice.

Have patience.) Then note whether the benefits are accompanied by any "downside" qualities. Is there any price to pay for the expression of the anger that you can see or that you anticipate could materialize? This of course involves speculation, but a sensitivity may exist that allows one to predict with some level of accuracy. This is an ability that can also be developed through practice. Keeping anecdotal notes can be most useful here—a triple list of anger and the positive/negative consequences associated with it.

Some anger-expressions can be complex in both purpose and results. For example, a politician might efficiently get votes by making voters angry or fearful, but might also create suspicion and hatred among the public, leading to dire results. The original goal was achieved, but the level of "success" is questionable.

Now watch for these same cues and clues in your own relationship to anger—whether you are emanating or receiving them. See how objective you can be in your observation of this very subjective action. Through this effort anger might become a useful teaching tool (as well as a useful tactical tool).

END-OF-CHAPTER QUESTIONS:

1. When do you first remember experiencing inner conflicts (as described in the story Middle School above)? Has the character of the conflicts changed as you have matured?
2. Do you have a sense of how you affect those around you—in general and at specific moments—friends, family, work peers, or acquaintances?
3. What might you add to the list of important techniques/skills to know for the classroom? As you observe yourself and your past actions, how much weight would you say you have given to these skills?

ANGER TOOLS

4. What other language skills would add strength to a teacher's repertoire of classroom abilities?
5. How might you help students become more aware of their own self-talk—both quiet and loud varieties?
6. How else do you play in the classroom? Do you seek new ideas from peers?
7. Have you employed anger effectively? How? Is this something you could pass on to others?

CHAPTER FIVE

CLASSROOM SETTING AND ANGER

"In the classroom, do not use anger when angry."
—Glenn Nystrup

THE HUMAN DESIRE TO LEARN

As human beings we hold a natural tendency that pushes us to learn and to grow. Simply observe a growing infant to verify. This process begins immediately, with the first breath—no conscious intention needed. Changes then occur to the natural desire to learn along the maturation path—some natural, some not. Physical change, emotional and intellectual development, and growing self-awareness are natural consequences of living a life.

Parents, teachers, and others, as they take their significant role in this growth process, might inspire or inhibit, with intention or not, and will

CLASSROOM SETTING AND ANGER

certainly set unexpected occurrences in motion. Even the simple desire to help and support can backfire if it is too extreme or carried on for too long.

In this chapter we consider aspects of the school environment which might contribute to an increase or decrease in a student's development and to acceptance or frustration on their part in the classroom.

E.G. — ON THE DURATION OF ONE'S SCHOOLING

John Taylor Gatto, three-time New York City Teacher of the Year, one-time New York State Teacher of the Year, and author of educational books—told a story about David G. Farragut, naval officer and renowned sea captain for the United States during the War of 1812 and the Civil War. Mr. Gatto remembered Farragut for his quote, "Damn the torpedoes, full steam ahead." Farragut was commissioned as *midshipman* when he was nine years old and *prize master* at the age of twelve. At twelve he was also asked to captain a captured ship back to port. To do so he had to defend against hardened sailors—his own crew members, who were on the verge of rebellion because they refused to serve under a twelve-year-old captain. He had to exert his authority and lead his crew safely to port. The story goes that one of these crusty old sailors went below-decks to get his weapons. He would not bow to such a young captain. "What shall we do, Captain?" others asked of Farragut. "If he comes up with his guns, shoot him," Farragut replied. The sailor did not come up with weapons as he realized his choice, which was to follow—and to live. Farragut did what he had to, with strength, assuming the greatest responsibility possible on that ship. And then Mr. Gatto states, "If David Farragut was in school [today] he would be in the seventh grade."

What do we ask of *our* seventh-graders?

Since schooling will be a way of life for children through many changes and growth stages, the difference between a passive engagement and active participation in their education will be essential. The longer they remain passive—told what to learn and when—the less able they will be in the navigating and piloting of their own lives.

A teacher, though not alone in this, is a primary factor in establishing the particular tone of a classroom and in shaping the setting. Whether done in accord with desired goals or in a more haphazard manner, whether selfless or selfish—the teacher is the one *in the trenches, in the front row, in the driver's seat*. Since the tone and setting in a classroom will then directly influence how smoothly the class operates and the well-being of each student, a teacher's actions will be critical here. We explore a selection of significant factors in the setting of tone in a classroom:

TRUST:

- I wish to develop a setting of trust—trust not only that a student can feel towards the teacher, but trust that I will have the student's best interest in mind and in heart.
- I wish to develop a setting of trust—trust that will hold beyond student transgressions or teacher errors—a two-way trust that is deeper than isolated behaviors—a trust that can act as a foundation for the student-teacher relationship.
- I wish to develop a setting of trust—trust that one can safely explore within the classroom environment topics discussed, ideas generated, interpersonal relationships, and the workings of oneself.
- I wish to develop a setting of trust—trust that I (student or teacher) can be different, and that is okay—trust that I can be different, and that is good—trust that I don't need to hide myself from others or from myself.

A lack of trust, in any of these areas, can feed into alienation, negativity, and anger.

CHAOS LEVEL:

As a teacher, I can't expect students to behave like perfect little order-followers—unless I wish to create robots devoid of initiative. I can expect instead to find some level of chaos, disorder, surprise, mistakes, and disturbance. Often I see this where high levels of learning are going on, where students are engaged in activities that on the surface look different from one another, where enthusiasm thrives and experimentation is rich. Often small disturbances will be seen, paths will be crossed, and emotional and physical bumps will occur—all part of the environment that welcomes the unexpected. Chaos could, however, be a sign of low levels of learning as well, where a teacher allows laziness to rule, and a haphazard atmosphere to exist. Learning then becomes accidental, and too often emotional disturbances replace enthusiasm and the eagerness to learn.

In a tolerant classroom I see that noise and activity levels increase and decrease, and order and cleanliness ebb and flow. I find that this non-rigid, chaotic, *contained bedlam* can be rich in learning and interactive experience. I see students confident enough to express themselves and to take risks. I watch with amusement as I quietly predict the outcome of Charlie's speech to Celeste, or Danny's surprise at his own success. Everywhere I look I see a different view of a class involved in deep interaction and exploration, of students working solo or overlapping action and conversation here and there, blending into a scene reminding me at times of a Fellini film.

As a teacher, whether it be of elementary, middle, or secondary school, I need to determine whether I have the capacity not only to exist in this type of environment, but to thrive in it as well. It is an environment rich with moments when students are engaged in varied activities, reacting to classroom material in different ways, interacting with each other in a wide variety of patterns and learning how to explore and express individuality. Voices might at times be raised and spills might occur.

To expect the behavior of students to remain within a tight and narrow framework is to expect students to place their primary effort and attention into pleasing the outside forces that pressure them, and not to explore a path of interest—an essential element of human learning and growth. Though uniformity has certain clear value and has its place in classroom schooling, constant constriction and strict uniformity is, at best, highly limiting—and at worst, oppressive and destructive.

As students advance through the grades, most schools expect increasingly more contained and restrained behavior. The activity discussed here, of periods of varied projects and explorations and of students engaging in substantive dialogue with each other and the teacher, does not conflict with this expectation. Exploration and self-guided action are essential for any age. After all, the ultimate goal of education is for self-guidance as students leave behind being students.

In the words of A L Staveley:

> *"It is difficult to find the right way to help a child toward an understanding that one suspects—with all too much reason—is missing in oneself. So willy-nilly we find ourselves teaching them to conform, to conceal, to lie, to fear adverse public opinion. In other words, in the jargon of the day, we 'socialize' them, and it is no wonder there are so many social wrecks. There is no more devastating tyrant than the community, as the ants themselves would no doubt have confirmed had they not been obliged after they finally achieved their perfect community, to give up everything, including sex and the gift of speech."* (1)

This acceptance of a moderate level of disorder at times in the classroom can lead to increased vibrancy and learning, when the teacher is able to monitor and guide the flow of the class. It can also, however, lead in another direction. If the chaos occurs due to teacher lack of interest or ability, the result is not pretty—devolution rather than evolution—things can go downhill fast. Ignorance is not the way. There must exist a thread of order within the chaos, so that students understand where the parameters exist regarding safety, respect, and necessary regulations.

The best locus for this perspective will rest within the students themselves—internalized, embraced.

Some of the scenes I most cherish in the classroom are when standing to the side and observing students in eager activity: building, talking, arguing, cooperating, competing, experimenting, failing, or smiling at small successes. I might need to put out a small flare-up between students here and there, or help when someone is stuck, or give support through words or tools. I, as teacher, am a facilitator rather than puppeteer.

These are perfect areas in which to observe how students deal with frustrations and conflicts and to offer support through individual, small group, or class-wide discussions. Here is where anger can be a natural springboard to students becoming better acquainted with their own tendencies, needs, and abilities. Here is where students can learn to stand in the face of unexpected moments and situations and practice maintaining a calm interior while the exterior is a swirl of action and fluctuation. The skills learned and used in order to remain comfortable in these situations are the same ones that will be of benefit when confronting anger—whether in oneself or in others—and also in facing up to life's many challenges.

It's a beautiful thing to find that thread of order that can run through a chaotic scene. A teacher who is practiced at this will be able to see it at work in a classroom or with any small group of children, if it's there. A teacher who is practiced will be able to foster or create the setting for this vibrant line of order running through the seeming chaos. When this order is in place it's a thread that's understood by many of the students in the class, and sensed by most. The scene becomes more fluid—guided rather than constricted—guided by the inner being of the students, with a quiet hand of a wise teacher.

EXERCISE 13:
Observing Effective Anger

Your chaos index—explore your personal perspective:
1. I look around the classroom and see order and quiet, the way I like it.
2. I get irritated when things go off course or off schedule.
3. I allow a level of noise and mixing it up at certain times during the day—at transition times but not during study time.
4. I most often try to keep order, but sometimes I just don't have the energy for it, and I let things slide.
5. I make the attempt to include **loose** time during subject studies (e.g., moving around and talking time for students, such as with small group projects).
6. I am clear with students about which behaviors are acceptable and which are not.
7. I waffle.

How to work with this theme:
1. Question yourself about what you might be comfortable with and what could work for you.
2. Observe yourself in action to see if your responses to Part 1 are consistent with your behavior and comfort level.
3. Set a plan for how you will structure this aspect of the daily classroom operation.
4. Follow your plan as well as you are able to for a set period (one or two weeks?).
5. Assess the success of your plan.
6. Adjust as necessary.

and reaching out—
7. Observe peers and others in action, looking for tolerance levels (intentional or accidental), techniques

for management, and/or styles of communication with students.
8. Discuss this topic with administration, peers, and others.

WHEN TO STEP IN:

Related to the theme above of *chaos*, is choosing *when to step in* to certain processes occurring in the classroom. There is so much that teachers are responsible for, so many areas of growth to monitor, that it would be impossible to control factors down to a minute level, and exhausting to even try. As teachers, we must choose where we place our effort and our influence.

One practice that might help alleviate some of the *control through planning* that teachers so consistently engage in is to offer more *choice* to students. This can be done with curriculum, medium, and assessment choices. It will likely require more time of the teacher in the beginning to set this up, but reduce needed time later, and may offer other rewards as well.

Students often become more engaged with the material and invested in results when they participate in curriculum decision. As Maryellen Weimer states in her November 2017 article, "When students make a decision, they're more likely to own it. Less blame can be put on the teacher if students don't like what they're learning. Making the decision about what to learn encourages students to accept more of the responsibility for learning."

Independence is another key target for students. This is what schools and teachers are aiming for—to help foster able, independent individuals—young adults who might take a fitting place in the adult world. Again, Maryellen Weimer: "Making content choices is part of what's involved in being an independent, self-directed learner. Mature learners decide what to learn when they discover there's something they need to know..." (2)

Making independent choices is essential for students at every age and grade, and may contribute to a passion for learning that is beyond something created by teachers. Teachers might facilitate it, guide it at times, but passion is something internal, within each of us. It might be fed, allowed to flourish, or suppressed by continuous direction from outside.

In her book, *Where is Bernardino*, A. L. Stavely makes a clear case for those working with the very young: "One of the hazards of working with very young children is the feeling you 'ought' to be teaching them something or other. You can't! They are learning so much and so fast that there is no room for teaching, except at the expense of the learning process. You can watch the learning, regulate it a little, enhance the existing opportunities for learning and introduce ones. That is about it. They absorb experiences and transform them into the material of their own being in much the same way that they transform food into their growing bodies." (3)

A teacher is constantly faced with classroom moments that demand a decision of how to engage, or even whether or not to engage. What criteria are employed in these decisions, what scale used? When attention is directly placed on the "why" and "how" of the decisions to intervene, a teacher might find that the intervention is not always needed, or that an entirely different path should be taken from the one planned.

The shifting of curriculum choice to students, will allow a teacher to *step back* and a student to *step forward* in being the decision-maker. Adjusting the way material is presented or how student work is assessed, can be areas of student self-guidance as well.

Knowing what the outcome goals of classroom activities and assignments are will be essential in determining how much intervention and guidance is necessary from the teacher. If outcome goals can be met while offering ever-decreasing dependence on the teacher, then students will be moving simultaneously toward the broad-sweeping goal of independence.

EXPERIENTIAL LEARNING:

There is no substitute for experiential learning— hands-on, heart-in, head-focused. When experience like this is occurring there is less room for boredom, disinterest, or frustration. Both short and long-term results may reveal rich, self-directed learning.

David Kolb's *experiential learning theory* describes learning:

> "Learning is the process whereby knowledge is created through the transformation of experience." (4).

It also includes an element of reflection (a form of self-observation, repeatedly emphasized in this book).

Being involved directly in an experience and having an experience described are two vastly different things. The *first* will include not only the mind, but also all of the sensing of the moment and the feelings engaged when our attention is present. This can be a deeply rich experience— multifaceted and multi-layered.

The *second*, learning through the verbal/visual description of an experience without direct experience (also referred to as *didactic* or *rote* learning), fails to reach the same dimension of learning because memory (a primary factor in understanding and retention) pales through this second method.

The more a student can have experiential learning, the more that particular learning can connect to other experiences and insights, providing enhanced understanding. Education of the first category is far more full, interesting, and usable.

When students are interested in their education, in what they are experiencing, there is less fertile ground for anger. When experience is rich, learning is rich, and memory gains depth and dimension. From this, students can more easily engage what they have learned—performing better in class on tests, and in more substantial life skills.

Developing the classroom setting through experiential learning is one of the basic ways to encourage interest and discourage anger. This holds true for students of any grade level, from kindergarten through post-secondary. Experiential learning can touch passion and unlock vibrant energy in each student.

STIMULATING CLASSROOM:

Teachers (and educational institutions) are increasingly recognizing the value of a stimulating classroom—where student learning, interest, and participation may be enhanced, and dampening aspects of the school experience (such as feelings of boredom and irrelevance) may be alleviated. "In a stimulating classroom, students are able to move around, learn new ways of receiving knowledge, and are encouraged to question everything around them. Because of this, it's easier for them to become involved in the learning process." Instructor: Amanda Wiesner-Groff (5)

Experiential learning, as discussed above, is a strong aspect of a stimulating classroom. A selection of other valuable aspects follows:

PHYSICAL SETTING

- An orderly space will contribute to orderly thinking.
- Create a classroom that is clean, colorful, and bright.
- Provide positive messaging (without being overly dramatic, cliche, or beneath age-level).
- Invite interaction (e.g., books and magazines to look at or read, art supplies available for lunch or recess time, board games).
- Display material related to current topics and curriculum.
- Consider classroom changes before stagnation sets in. Rotate posters, magazines, interesting objects.
- Interest areas in the classroom might work at many grade-levels.

CIRRICULUM & CIRRICULUM DELIVERY

- Provide novel experiences through methods of delivery and engagement (e.g., debates over court cases or historical events).
- Include visual and hands-on learning. (See Chapter Four, Techniques.)

CLASSROOM SETTING AND ANGER

- Offer choice of curriculum where possible or have students help establish method of delivery of curriculum.
- Make links to the larger world around "how does the class-work relate?" For example, "Why math?"—or "How does science hurt or help us?"— or a bit more provocative, such as "Is science the ultimate arena of knowledge?"

CLASSROOM HABITAT

- Provide clear delineations (lines in the sand). Help students know where it's okay to play around and stretch boundaries and where it is not, such as with: personal insults, oppressive behavior, unsafe actions, and/or activity detrimental to class learning or wellbeing.
- Be clear and direct with language, voice, and action. Help students understand the difference between a teacher deliberately adapting a stance and a "zero-tolerance" situation.
- Allow movement. Encourage movement around the room through activities and policies.
- Create periodic change in the interactive setting. (e.g., In graduate classrooms I would often change the desk arrangements into rows, small clusters, or one great circle—even during the course of one class—so that at times I could be at the same physical level as the students.)
- Encourage collaboration, an important skill for most professions.
- Engage students through questioning, higher-order thinking, and independent inquiry.
- Help Students determine how they engage with material (e.g., drama; analysis; write a paper, play, or skit; write a song or rap) to show what they know.
- Develop ways for students to teach other students, and build it into the curriculum.
- Employ music, video, and other art forms.
- Explore *mindfulness* in its various manifestations—to find one appropriate for the class.

TEACHER

- Learn in front of your students (e.g., new vocabulary, new links to related issues or information).
- Observe interaction. Act as resource versus holder of strict form, fun versus "the great critic." Show appreciation of error and exploration.
- Show interest and exuberance. Love the subject and what you do.
- Engage students by name (when the timing is appropriate).
- Admit "I don't know," or "I just learned this recently," or "I was excited to discover this."
- Express appreciation of student efforts and willingness to take risks.
- Join students in activities—write, draw, read.
- Laugh— have fun. It's okay.
- Be real. Show that you are human, and deal with issues as *they* must—that you learn how and appreciate the opportunity to do so.
- Provide frequent positive feedback.
- Hold high expectations for students and set challenging standards.

Much dissatisfaction, leading toward anger, might be avoided in the school setting through students feeling that they belong in the classroom they are in and that there is welcome engagement for them there. Emphasis of this might be found in the following statement from a novel Israeli school: . "A dynamic and constantly changing reality requires adaptation and change in educational approaches: the student is no longer to be seen as a passive receptacle for knowledge, but as an active participant in the construction of knowledge. This approach requires a substantial change in the teaching process and it challenges the traditional hierarchical teacher-student relations as well as the physical learning environment." (6)

DISCIPLINE WITHOUT THE "DIS":

One of the more interesting *slang* words I've come across is the elevation of the prefix "dis" to stand alone and to carry its own meaning. With its central meaning of "*to put one down*" the wide array of possible words to fit makes this slang widely versatile. *Dis* could replace: disrespect, disparage, distance, disturb, distract, distress, dislocate, dismember, disgorge, disintegrate, or disarm—any of which can feel mightily uncomfortable. Simultaneously, more than one word/meaning of *dis* can fit a particular communication, written or verbal.

The goal here is to use *dis*cipline with students without them feeling that they are being *dissed*. To retain respect for students while simultaneously playing the role of disciplinarian is a most valuable skill, worthy of an accomplished teacher. Some of us will naturally have greater ability at this than others. All of us can improve.

A teacher holds respect for students, even in a situation where discipline is needed, by monitoring her *inner stance*. This is the position from which she looks out at the world at any particular moment. A position of: "What can I do to help this student and this situation?" is radically different from: "How can I control this student and this unwanted behavior?" "I am the teacher and I am the one who knows what is needed here" is very different from, "I listen for the truth in each comment, no matter who it comes from, or how angry I might feel at the moment." (See Chapter Four, "What Language Do You Speak?".)

Inner stance is something that can be cultivated. It can change and mature in a person. A choice is before us: passively accept that the way we see things is simply *the way it is* and there is no need or possibility to change anything or actively monitor and assess our viewpoints, prejudices, and opinions. We can become static and identified with the views that we have picked up *along the way* in our life, or we can look with an eye to growing portions of our inner stance—as we choose. The act of monitoring the feelings and attitude that we hold when engaged in discipline is a good way to begin. (See Chapter Two, Changing Perspective.)

EXERCISE 15:
Inner Stance

Our inner workings are not static—as we have observed through many pages of this book. We can initiate and influence change— breaking some of the accidentally acquired bondage that constricts us. Consider:
- Do you employ discipline without holding a dismissive or condescending view?
- How can you strengthen your ability to do this?
- When are you unable or unwilling to make this effort to hold the other individual with such an intention—with respect and appreciation? What are your "trigger" points?
  - Specific words spoken
  - Lack of respect
  - A repeat-offender with whom you have lost patience
  - An unwillingness to meet you halfway
  - Personality conflicts
  - Your low energy or sour mood
  - Other person not deserving of your forgiveness
  - Other

Now see what you can do to shape your inner stance, your attitude, your perspective. To begin, manage your outer words and actions, employing the philosophy, "Act as if..." until the effort becomes more internalized and ingrained in you. Act as if you truly care, and simultaneously try to find that actual feeling within you. Do this repeatedly.

At the same time, when negative or contrary thoughts occur like, "This is stupid." or "Why am I doing this?"— acknowledge their presence and say to yourself, "No thank you, not right now, I have work to do." Personal growth in areas such as this can be challenging, yet quite energizing and strengthening, as well.

CLASSROOM SETTING AND ANGER

THE CLASSROOM DANCE:

The *Classroom Dance* is often difficult to define or put to words, yet it's not so difficult to sense whether the "dance" is *working* or *not working*.

E.G. — WHAT IS GRAVITY?

I felt my feet on the floor, the air temperature on my skin. A dozen pairs of eyes looked directly at me, waiting, expecting. Thoughts swirled through this brain. I let them swirl. None had the gravity to hold my attention. None were needed. The subject today actually was about *gravity* and laws of science and Mr. Newton. I allowed this thought to enter, to take center stage. I often begin with a question or provocative statement—a simple one today. "What is gravity?" We then looked at the responses offered by the students. We looked for accuracy (if there actually was *one* source of *accurate*). We categorized responses (e.g., "Is that a definition or description or example of..."). We looked at what Sir Isaac himself had to say. And on we travelled.

All the while I watched the attentiveness and interest level of each student, interaction between students, and their falling into usual personal habits. I watched eyes and would adjust the action of my hands or other props to attract them. I would rephrase, repeat, or reveal information in order for them to grasp and appreciate the lesson. If an opportunity came up to move tangentially into related areas, or to provide a valuable vocabulary lesson, I would jump on it—knowing that I would soon lead the discussion back to the main lesson. I might veer off to travel with a personal story someone just offered, or a topic just mentioned, or a film they all might be familiar with—keeping interest, showing respect, and simply having fun.

I might then add a provocative question to invite thinking outside the ordinary, such as "If you were placed in the very center of the earth, how much would you weigh?" An interesting discussion usually follows as students formulate their personal responses. What do you think, reader?

This is all part of the dance—the swing to the side, the hop to the back, the dip forward. - We can all go on a "joyride," or have serious discussion, or "buckle-down" and work. The classroom dance could take us many places and remain entirely appropriate—if we can hear the music (the classroom vibration, the group connection). Or we can feel completely out of step. How we develop as teachers and as individuals will determine this.

BE AWARE!

Any of these more subtle connections to students and to the energy in a classroom will be enhanced with mastery of concrete basics such as curriculum material. A struggle with the basics will leave little room for subtle, nuanced interaction with students.

END-OF-CHAPTER QUESTIONS:

1. How can you picture students gaining important life experience while spending so much of their vital waking time in classrooms?
2. Is *trust* a strong component of your classroom structure? How?
3. How might you define *chaos*, *loose structure*, and *student engagement*? Is there a difference—in look, in feel, in learning for you or the students?
4. How controlling are you in the classroom? Do students get much chance to lead? Is this intentional?
5. What is one thing you do in your classroom that would be described as experiential learning? What is one more thing you could add?
6. In your experience as a student, name five things that you would

include in the category of *stimulating classroom*. What subject areas were these? What was the teacher like?

7. Place four of your past teachers on a scale running from discipline without *dis*, to discipline with plenty of it. Describe how it felt to you.

CHAPTER SIX

CLASSIFIED

"Speak when you are angry—and you'll make the best speech you'll ever regret."
—Laurence J. Peter

SPECIAL EDUCATION AND ANGER:

Students who find themselves in the world of special education often face difficulty upon difficulty. In addition to learning, physical, or social challenges, anger may be a frequent visitor. Frustration at an inability to communicate with ease can lead to myriad difficulties. Sensitivity to teasing and bullying may be heightened. Simply having to deal with a handicap or challenge can bring on a rush of anger and a sense of separation. Students with high-functioning Autism Spectrum Disorder (h-f ASD) [once called Asperger Syndrome (AS)], Traumatic Brain Injury (TBI), Attention Deficit Hyperactive Disorder (ADHD), Emotional Behavioral Disorder (EBD), Post-traumatic Stress Disorder (PTSD), and more all are susceptible to various intensities of anger. Helping them to prevent the onset of anger and to react appropriately once gripped by anger, is the job of every teacher, counselor, and school administrator.

Special education is a branch of teaching that is at play in nearly every school that exists. Individuals with special needs are found throughout society, at every level and location. Ranging widely in intellectual, emotional, and physical abilities, special-ed (special-education) students, like general-ed (general-education) students, may make great contributions to society, bring considerable trouble upon themselves and others, or inhabit the range between.

Special education, in fact, exists only in comparison to a general-education population, or "norm", from which the special-education students stand out. Hence, the manner in which the "norm" is defined will determine the definition of special education. For example, a student who is very active and is required to sit passively at a desk in a school setting for several hours each day will likely be placed in the category of special education. In a ranch or large sea-craft setting, however, that same student might stand out as a stellar achiever, while a student who is able to sit passively all day would be considered a special-needs person. What we need then is some form of common definition or vocabulary, such as by Daniel P. Hallahan et al. in *Exceptional Learners*:

> *"Special education means specially designed instruction that meets the unusual needs of an exceptional student."* (1)

and:

> *"For purposes of education, exceptional learners are those who require special education and related services if they are to realize their full human potential."* (2)

This sets a lofty goal for education—"...to realize their full human potential." This, essentially, is the goal for all education—at least to make steps along the way. Many individuals will spend a lifetime pursuing this goal for themselves or for others. What can we, as teachers, do to further this goal in each of our students? Let's explore.

The topic of special education is huge. We will look at a selection of aspects that relate to our theme of *anger in the classroom*. In doing so we'll focus on three common classifications that can be found within the field of special education: ASD, ADHD, and EBD.

Some areas where anger often shows itself in regards to school issues may be outside of the classroom directly, and outside the scope of this book. An example would be the controversy regarding "full inclusion." This concerns the placement of students with a wide range of special needs into general education classrooms. This is a hot topic, and much anger can materialize on both sides of the debate. But it's the students within the classroom that concern us here.

FAIR VERSUS EQUAL

One of the basic tenets of special education—one that is misunderstood by many teachers, administrators, and parents—is the concept of what is "fair" in education. As we see in the definition above, special education holds the intention of offering all students an equal opportunity to succeed, regardless of their learning style or condition.

This does *not* mean that every student is to be treated in an exact, same, prescribed manner. It means that each student is to be given an equal opportunity according to his/her specific needs and abilities, within a reasonable measure. In some cases it is this basic concept that is not understood and the feeling is that all students must be treated exactly the same, without allowance for any differences. With this approach, special-needs students would not receive special treatment and there would be no individualization in a classroom. In other cases it's the last part of the above statement, "within a reasonable measure," that is argued. Just when should extra help be offered, and when should it be let go?

E.G. — ADA

I had suggested to the teacher of a girl I tutored, Ada, that she be given special tasks or responsibilities that would allow her to move about during each school day. Ada was not a trouble-maker, but her need to move, when constricted, did cause trouble in the classroom. The teacher responded, "I can give her special tasks but they would only happen once a week since I will need to make sure that all of the children in class have a chance to do these same tasks. It's only fair."

But is this *fair*, or is it *equal*? In this case, to treat every child in an equal way meant that the child in need did not get a fair chance, but was at a disadvantage due to her inherent characteristics. What could have been a simple solution instead remained a problem—for the child, and for everyone in the classroom—as behavior became difficult. The teacher could not see the difference between fair and equal in this case. Sometimes being *fair* is not *equal*, and being treated *equally* is not *fair*.

EXERCISE 16:
Treated Differently

Take note, where possible, of inclusion settings where special ed students are given different treatment from fellow students. Record what factors are involved that you can see? Does the special treatment appear to be methodical and planned ahead, or a response to a particular moment? Does the special treatment attract much attention from other students? Is it distracting to them—or to the teacher? Is this a co-teaching situation, and do the teachers seem to be in agreement, working collaboratively? There are many things to see when observing special treatment of students. Consider these factors—and others you might add:
- Does the special treatment seem effective?
- Do any (or all) parties involved appear distracted or annoyed?

- Does the student appear to be affected socially or emotionally by the special focus?
- Can you tell what the purpose of the special help is?
- Are extra personnel needed to accomplish the special treatment?
- How much preparation do you think is needed to accomplish the intended goals?
- What would happen if no special treatment was offered? How might the situation differ?

GIVING STUDENTS AN OUT:

Giving students an "out" relates to all special ed classification, and indeed would best be available in some form to every school student.

An essential aspect of any program addressing strong student emotions is to provide them with an outlet for build-up pressures—to *vent* or *let off steam*. An effective approach could vary from student to student, relative to timing, personality, setting, etc. At the same time there might be a number of universal approaches to success. While one student might benefit from a short scream (when the situation is appropriate) another might benefit most from a quiet, meditative moment. Yet, both will be helped by having avenues for release of built-up pressure, and knowing clearly what those options might be.

PREPARING AHEAD OF TIME

Help students explore social topics that affect them. Offer class discussions presenting scenarios and topics appropriate to the experience of the students (e.g., bullying, social or academic frustrations, feeling out of place) or student- generated topics. Initiate individual discussions with specific students (e.g., "How will you handle [situation/issue]?").

Model your own experience. Speak of certain challenges you face as a teacher—as a person.

DISCUSS THE "LOOK" OF THINGS

Saving face—A conversation might include something like the following:

Walking away from a conflict will often be considered a last resort. "If I walk away I'll look weak.! I'll be giving in to my adversary and I don't like the way it'll look or feel."

The tendency might instead be to defend—to defend at all costs. In such a situation objectivity is lost, and decisions will literally be out of my control. Emotions and imagination will rule.

However, if I am able to bring reason into the mix and not proceed solely on emotional reaction, I might actually see that the stronger approach is to walk away from the interaction and not fear how I'll look. Inner strength will be sufficient to take such an action. The weaker position will be the inability to even consider the act of walking away.

This could present an uncomfortable contradiction: walking away might be the real strength, and look weak, while staying in conflict might be the weak approach, yet look stronger—at least in our self-imagining.

SELF-RIGHTEOUSNESS

Combatting a sense of self-righteousness can be very difficult. "I am right, the other party is wrong, and I will sure as hell make this clear," may be an inner voice loudly demanding our attention. At the same time a gut reaction may be saying, "This doesn't feel right. Yes I see that I'm upset but my reacting doesn't feel appropriate."

This conflict in our feelings may serve as a useful reminder that choices can be made. We need not merely slide down the well-worn ruts (routes) we have created over a life-time. We might recognize a mature response. It might be difficult to take a more reasoned approach, or to shift our feelings toward the other party involved, but the ability to open up these possibilities to ourselves will offer us greater ease and effectiveness.

PLAN OF ACTION

Any plan of action would best be clearly understood by both student and teacher. If there is not consistency and clarity between the two, then the success of the plan is doubtful and could instead lead to mistrust or unwillingness to try again.

E.G. — BRAD

Brad was a middle school student who would at times look at an assignment, a math sheet for example, and quickly get enraged if it looked too difficult for him—enraged at the assignment and at himself for his "incompetence." He would tear it up, leave the room, and be unapproachable for half an hour, at the least. We did learn, both of us, how to better deal with this particular scenario, though other things could still set him off. At one point I said to him, "I know that sometimes you get angry and it's best for you to not be in the classroom at that time. I'll try, but I won't always see the exact right thing to do. You have my permission to leave the classroom if you determine that it's necessary. Just take yourself away from the situation if you feel that it's something you need to do. You don't need my permission to leave. The smart thing at that point *is* for you to leave, and I expect that sometimes you'll know that better than I will."

One day soon after, I said "no" to his leaving the room during a group lesson when he asked to. It appeared that he might be using our recent discussion as an excuse to get out of work. Two minutes later Brad left anyway, with some signs of being upset. I felt a ping of anger at myself regarding his leaving. After ten minutes, when I had a moment, I found him holed up behind a door (his usual spot)—angry, ready for a blast from me.

At that point I said, "Brad you did great, thank you for leaving when you did, for seeing what you needed and then acting on it. When you're ready, come back to the classroom." Then I left, but not before I could see his shoulders loosen a bit. He was back in the room in five minutes. For him it was record time. We said no more about it, just picked up from there. Any other lessons would be completely unimportant at the time and liable to interfere with this particularly effective one. The value here is that this young man just learned directly about self-control and self-direction—a lesson that could be of immense value in many new settings. The math could wait.

RESOURCES: LINE UP YOUR SUPPORTS

Ask students, "Who would you like to go see now, so that you can calm down?"

A couple of cautions are in order here:

—Determine as best possible whether or not this student feigns or allows anger to escalate in order to get to a favored place like the gym. Perhaps the special visit can take place after a calm-down period.

—Know what resources are available. Interview school personnel—all coaches, teachers, and administrators are potentials. Which do you think might be responsive? Then check with students during particular moments of need.

—Help students determine sources of support for varied issues, including conflicts with others; internal conflicts; or powerful, disruptive emotions. Be as specific as possible about which source can help with what particular issue. It is up to the teacher to compile a list and to communicate with various service providers to determine their best areas of support, such as:

- Guidance counselors
- Specialized teachers or staff
- Other teachers from the school
- Peers

- Administrators
- Coaches
- Individuals from the community with social or religious affiliations

Support can take many forms. It might mean someone to talk to, a place to blow off steam such as a gym, or simply a space in which to be quiet. Providing opportunity for students to meet various potential support personnel (in an official capacity or not) can help build the link for students when it is needed.

Other considerations:
- How can I help students to appropriately self-advocate?
- How can I help students determine when to self-advocate?
- Are the resources currently in place for students appropriate or enough?
- What new supports need to be put into place?

Questions for students to ask of themselves:
- What does the school administration expect of me?
- What support can I expect from administration, peers, teachers, specialists?
- What am I good at, and how can I use this to support others and myself?
- What do I wish to improve or learn in regards to supports and resources for me?

Directly working with students in developing answers to these questions can stimulate valuable discussions and arm students with potential solutions to difficult situations. The very act of including students in discussions such as this can stimulate knowledge of and confidence in themselves.

Consider also that many supports can be found and established outside of the school. Community supports of many kinds exist, both private and public. These are supports that might be appropriate for students in crisis or supports for an entire classroom, such as spending a couple of hours a week gardening in a community setting or helping build a town dog park. These activities may then be incorporated into class lessons linking the practical with the theoretical. Other supports might be directly focused on hot issues such as bullying or prejudice. Many opportunities exist.

ASD (AUTISTIC SPECTRUM DISORDER) AND ASPERGER SYNDROME (AS)

Asperger Syndrome (AS), once a stand-alone classification, is a special ed category that has been absorbed into the Autistic Spectrum Disorder (ASD) classification in the DSM-5 (Diagnostic and Statistical Manual of Mental Disorders, Fifth Edition—a.k.a. DSM-5 as of 2013. (3) Before this date, AS and AD (Autism Disorder) were both considered subcategories of Pervasive Developmental Disorders (PDD). ASD is the name for a group of developmental disorders which includes a wide range, "a spectrum," of symptoms, skills, and levels of disability. For the sake of clarity and distinction I will refer to the former AS classification as high-functioning ASD (h-f ASD), indicating where this set of characteristics would be placed on the spectrum.

The h-f ASD identification is characterized by a collection of traits found in common in a number of individuals. These traits, such as difficulty reading social cues, were separately noticed by two individuals— Leo Kanner in the United States and Hans Asperger in Austria. Both studied these groups of children and young adults, mostly boys, who shared certain behaviors and idiosyncrasies. Also interesting, as often happens in the fields of science and medicine for example—their discoveries were made at around the same time (1943-1944), independently, in different countries. Another common ground for these two men was that they both used the word "autistic" in their description (which had been used earlier in the twentieth century—deriving from the Greek "autos," meaning self). Both Kanner and Asperger were born in Vienna, as well, although Kanner lived in the US and conducted his studies there.

The autism spectrum can range from low-functioning nonverbal individuals; to high-functioning individuals; to *savants*, who may display abilities in selected areas that go far beyond the norm. Many famous people, and those who have shaped history, art, science, and more, are thought to have shared in these characteristics. Related information can be found online.

Individuals with h-f ASD characteristics are not a homogeneous group. There will be wide variability among them yet enough similarities to be able to characterize this population. Such individuals often display average or above intelligence. For this reason it is important that they work with a grade-appropriate curriculum in schools, and get accommodations as needed. The following is a selection of additional traits that *may* be associated with h-f ASD—(if enough of the characteristics apply to an individual, then she/he may be considered as included in this classification):

- Difficulty relating to others in a "normal" manner
- Problems with communication (often interprets language literally)
- Difficulty reading social cues (language/ facial or body cues)
- Keen interest in selected areas to the exclusion of others (often tries to steer conversation back to the selected area of interest or expertise)
- May have a somewhat flat, monotone voice, or rigid mannerisms
- May display under or over-stimulation to environment
- Strict adherence to routine or rules (or conversely, ignores them)

Struggle with irritability, frustration, prejudice, isolation, anxiety, or depression can lead these individuals to anger at many turns in their lives. Success at school, work, or in marriage can be difficult if they are not prepared to handle their particular character and characteristics.

I have witnessed h-f ASD students become angered when they are unable to conform to others' desires and pressures, or unable to make sense of subtleties surrounding cultural norms. Compounding this, it can be difficult for them to express themselves appropriately and to get their message across—whether angry or not. Communication and intimacy can be difficult.

Another level of anger can come from simply having to deal with being different, from having a "condition." "Why me? Why must I deal with all of this?" These students might as easily react negatively to being associated with other individuals who might look different—outside the norm. "Stop looking like a *tard*," I have heard some shout at classmates who share the same classification regarding a behavior such as a slight rocking back and forth—not wanting to be associated with this type of display.

Anger may also be used by these students as a buffer zone to keep others at bay to create distance—not wanting them close in order to avoid further confusion or hurt—or to reject the others before they themselves can be rejected. I have seen anger used to manipulate the individual's environment toward a singular focus, such as getting out of gym class or acquiring a new video game. I have seen other individuals simply wanting their condition to go away.

The comfort zone for these individuals is often smaller than for many of us, and the fear and discomfort of being outside of this zone can be far greater. What is considered normal in society and how they fit into that "normal" can be difficult as well. They often lack the perspective to notice how their behavior looks to others. Some individuals with h-f ASD have a slow processing speed and are at a disadvantage when a quick response is needed or when they compare themselves to others. This can also leave them feeling frustrated.

The "Hidden Curriculum" that many of us pick up naturally, by observing ourselves and others interact, can be elusive for these individuals. How to adjust one's behavior for different teachers, what not to say to certain students, what particular actions or expressions from others might mean, or where not to hang out on the playground, can be completely missed. This has the potential to present many frustrating, confusing, or even dangerous scenarios.

Individuals with h-f ASD sometimes don't have a wide choice of effective strategies when confronted with frustrations, strong emotions, or difficult situations. They rely on what they know (as all of us do). Yet, their pool of options can be far smaller than it is for others. Let's look now at some ways we might help them know more:

SEARCH FOR THE SOURCE OF ANGER

Finding the source of anger in h-f ASD students may help open a conversation and provide understanding about what is best to do next. I knew a boy named Tom who shouted, "I hate old people" when a group of elderly were near. He often said and did things that appeared on the surface aimed at offending or irritating others. As I looked deeper into this situation, however, I learned that two older family members had died within the prior year, and what Tom really hated was that old people died. We were able to have a discussion about this. It was short, but valuable.

Note—this is not about psychoanalysis or other in-depth inquiry. If the source of the anger is not within an easy search it may be best to let that effort go and focus more on how to affect stimulus-response for the student. If deeper help is needed, there are other sources for this.

WATCH FOR MISINTERPRETATIONS

Billy made a friendly overture to another student, offering a look at his new remote-controlled car. This friendly move, actually quite generous on Billy's part, was quite out of character between these two boys—so the receiver, David, could not recognize it. He simply said, "No." David did not understand the social impact of his response, and Billy was furious, ready to pummel David. After months of antagonism toward David, Billy finally made an effort to be nice to him—and was rejected. It was good that I was in the room.

HELP STUDENTS UNDERSTAND HOW THEIR ACTIONS AFFECT OTHERS

In the above story David did not understand what a rejection it was for Billy to be snubbed. Whatever the reason was that made David say "no" didn't matter to Billy. I have never seen David interested in cars before, and it would not be surprising if he did not trust Billy much. David said what he felt, as students with h-f ASD often do. In this interaction subtleties didn't come to bear.

With increased understanding of a situation such as this, these students might extrapolate their learning to similar situations and avoid numerous problematic interactions. And often this ability, of anticipating how another might feel or respond to one's words and actions, will need to be directly taught, more than once. In this case David and Billy were in a school tailored specifically to this type of learning.

HELP STUDENTS DEVELOP STRATEGIES

Some students with stronger conditions and unable to "read" certain settings well, might be taught set responses to specific situations. A typical example might be during the act of greeting someone. A student might learn to extend a hand and say, "Hello. My name is _____. Pleased to meet you." I have often seen this behavior, and it is clearly presented in the movie, "Temple Grandin" (an excellent film for anyone interested in learning about h-f ASD—with a superb performance by Claire Danes as Temple). This behavior can immediately start off a connection well by showing respect and providing the h-f ASD individual with an appropriate action plan. It will also express much to the person being greeted.

E.G. — TELLING JOKES

In the book *Elijah's Cup*, Valerie Paradiz speaks of her son's love of telling jokes. He would put strangers off, however, by running up to them saying, "Why did the chicken cross the road?." Valerie taught him to first ask, "Would you like to hear a joke?"

Then a yes or no response would tell him what to do next. (4) Simple—effective.

HELP STUDENTS KNOW WHAT IS APPROPRIATE AND WHAT IS NOT—

This is one of those overarching practices that is true for everyone, every age, everywhere - and it is especially true for h-f ASD students, where the understanding of subtlety and nuance might be weak. Help students learn how to ask questions of themselves and how to find answers—to questions such as:

- How can we tell what the other person wants during an interaction?
- How do we know when the expression of anger might be appropriate and when it is going too far? How do we know when we are alienating others around us?
- What are my goals at any particular moment, and are my actions moving me further from or closer to those goals?

E.G. — SECURITY

I once spoke with the director of security at a four-year college. She said that she was going to have to further address an issue with a young man who was following a young woman around campus. He was classified with AS (at the time), but that didn't change how he would be treated at a certain point. He began to follow the woman, who was friendly to him, around campus. She had been polite and friendly but did not want to explore the relationship further. By following her around, the young man felt that he was expressing his care for her. He felt that he was being polite and demonstrative. The director said she hoped that with further explanation the young man would understand that what he was doing was not acceptable, or she would be forced to treat him according to a different definition.

BE AWARE OF WHAT A STUDENT NEEDS RIGHT AFTER AN ANGRY EPISODE

Some of the students with AS that I have had the pleasure to work with would hold on to anger for extended periods once they fell into the grips of it. It was difficult for them to leave it behind. Those around them would attempt to create the best setting for the melting of the anger that gripped these students.

For one person it would mean giving wide berth and private space. For another it might mean engaging in lighthearted banter and activity. For another it could be some kind of discussion or analysis that works best. Some students barely remembered that an angry event even happened, quickly moving on and paying it no attention. Again we witness the diversity of character.

HELP THEM EXPAND THEIR "COMFORT ZONE"

This is something that most individuals could benefit from. For the h-f ASD student, expanding comfort zone might function on a social-survival level as well.

This expanding process might best begin with a clear picture of the comfort zone limits that are bumped into—of seeing the limits and vocalizing about them. Without this picture, little movement can be made. Then slowly and deliberately the limits and the tolerance can be pushed outward. For the most effective results, include the student herself in the process as much as possible.

Participation can help identify the issue at hand—determining goals for change, developing a plan of action, carrying out the plan, and assessing its success. The more frequent the participation, the stronger the results for the students. They come to *own* it—to accept and value it.

Recall the case-story about Donny in Chapter Four, *Techniques*. Donny expanded his *comfort* zone by clearly decreasing his *discomfort* zone.

PROVIDE A SAFE SPACE

There are times when the ability for an individual to escape from an overwhelming or highly stressful situation can be invaluable. It can provide a calming avenue for a troubled student and help prevent further escalation of anger or danger in the classroom. But a *safe space* will not work if the student is not engaged and in agreement with the activity or location offered. Preparation ahead of time is essential, along with assistance where needed. (See story about Brad at the beginning of this chapter, *Giving Students an Out*.)

ENGAGE THE STUDENT IN ABC RECORDINGS

ABC recording is a very effective method of allowing and encouraging a student to grow out of difficult behavioral patterns. The ABC here refers to Antecedent-Behavior-Consequence. Students can be provided with a log sheet or a diary where information can be recorded about incidents of felt or expressed anger, for example, along with notation about what came before and what happened after.

To help both teacher and student see whether the student recording is accurate, a period of tandem recording may be useful, where both student and teacher keep notes then compare them at set times. The teacher then withdraws support as the student shows competence. This is known as a *scaffolding approach*. The student in this case may then see what the teacher determines to be valuable notes, considering the goals of the effort.

In addition, the teacher gets to see what is deemed of value to the student. Here we see the importance of a teacher maintaining an open stance, so that learning might follow for her as well. An attitude of "I know—I teach" differs considerably from "What is occurring right now—what might I learn?" (For more on ABC, see Chapter Six on EBD.)

HELP STUDENTS WITH PRAGMATICS

Pragmatics refers to the way language is used in social settings, dealing more with the function of language than the mechanics of it. This is an area that can be tricky for students with h-f ASD. Idioms and colloquialisms can be quite confusing. With many h-f ASD students, the understanding of language leans more toward the literal rather than the subtle or nuanced. Miscommunication becomes an all-too-frequent result.

Noticing our own use of idioms or slang can help us see how much of this actually occurs in daily conversation. Often this occurrence is surprisingly high to anyone who makes the effort and is actually able to notice. Much of this indirect language is spoken automatically, without awareness. We say it and hear it without noticing. Increased awareness of our own use of such language offers a possibility of directly helping students with h-f ASD to better understand.

Creating or purchasing games and activities around idioms or communication might be of value as well—and fun.

EXERCISE 17:
Idioms—"As I Live and Breathe"

> Set times for yourself to record the use of idioms and similar figures of speech—by yourself and by others. I suggest that, at the start, you make your effort last through the morning hours. Let go of the activity at noon. As you practice this you might begin to catch other occurrences of idioms being spoken. You train the ear of your mind this way.
>
> Consider then how each phrase heard might be interpreted by someone who relies primarily on literal meaning.
>
> How might this influence understanding and overall communication?

E.G. — GRADUATE TASK

>I often gave this same assignment to graduate students I instructed who were on the path to becoming special ed teachers. I participated in each exercise that I assigned as well. One surprise for me was not how much I used idioms in my speech (since I practiced not speaking them, having worked with many students with *AS*) but how often idioms entered my thoughts. Idioms were regular visitors in the voice of my mind. The surprise was that I had not taken notice of them before this effort was made, even though I was practiced at not verbalizing them. I then began to wonder if these idioms had an effect on *how* I thought. Do idioms guide my thinking in subtle ways? I will continue to ponder and to observe this.

HELP THEM PREPARE FOR DIFFICULT TRANSITIONS

Change can be difficult for students with h-f ASD, even small changes. Transitions are often some of the most challenging times in schools for any students, as most teachers know. These moments of change can be amplified for the h-f ASD students—ranging from lesser changes like switching from one subject to the next, to greater changes, like attending a new school. Let's look at an example of one of the most difficult changes for these students, one that includes many large as well as small transitions.

Transitioning to a new school can be confusing and disturbing for any student, especially when making the change to middle school where students take on considerably more individual responsibility and have to work through far greater numbers of transitions each day. On top of this are the changes happening to students physically and emotionally as they become teens. For the h-f ASD student, many anxieties can arise at the enormity of it all. Here are possible actions that might alleviate some of the stress.

- For some students with h-f ASD, having a new teacher can be stressful. It could be very helpful for the student to meet the teacher before the beginning of the new school year, perhaps at the end of the prior year. If this isn't possible, then a communication from the teacher, accompanied by a photo, could be quite helpful. If some simple description of the teacher, such as some hobbies or other likes, could be given to the student as a welcome, he might feel more familiarity and more at ease. If the school-move is to a grade where there are to be numerous teachers, then this might be accomplished with the homeroom teacher, other willing teacher, or guidance counselor, for example.

- The opportunity to actually visit the new school ahead of time, before classes begin, can go a long way toward setting a student at ease. Especially where a student must change rooms several times a day, a map of the school will help. With this the student could navigate from homeroom to the office, to the lunchroom, to the gymnasium, to her locker, and to other classrooms—learning the location of them all. Help her as needed to begin with, then let her travel on her own, becoming familiar with the school layout. She'll have enough new information to deal with when school begins without adding *feeling lost* to complicate it all.

- When the school-year begins, one particularly difficult transition occurs when the bell rings. At this point the mass of humanity in the school is on the move and the intensity of the several-minute blast of energy and chaos between classes can cause great stress. (I have taught non-classified students in private schools who were there mainly because they couldn't handle the drama and stress of these transition periods in public schools.) At this point a buddy can be assigned to the h-f ASD student to help him navigate these transitions and to give support. Or the student might be allowed to leave five minutes early in order to get to his locker and then on to his next destination before the bell rings. He can be waiting outside his next classroom for easy entry after it empties.

If leaving early makes the student feel singled out and appear needy, he might be assigned a job such as bringing a copy of class attendance to the office. This way he has a legitimate reason for leaving early. Be aware that transitions can be the most confusing and troubling times—not ideal times for teachers to put students *out-of-mind* as they walk out of the classroom.

The above list is meant to provide examples of what might be done to help alleviate some of the stress that is built into an average school day. This stress becomes amplified for many students with special needs and can lead to problems for the student and the school. Frustration, stress, and confusion can all lead to increased levels of anger and acting out. Yet, with consideration and some simple actions, much of it can be avoided. Be creative and anticipate the needs of these students who might act and process information differently.

EBD (EMOTIONAL OR BEHAVIORAL DISORDER)

Defining Emotional or Behavioral Disorder (EBD) can be a difficult task. EBD is a difficult thing to measure or quantify and there can be overlaps with a number of other challenges. When it comes to definition, experts often disagree. Many groups and individuals resort to creating their own working definition for EBD. Following are some basic characteristics that are generally agreed upon, and will provide us with a place to begin our discussion. Challenges involve:

- Behavior that is chronic, often present, and difficult to stop
- Behavior that goes too far—goes to an extreme
- Behavior that is frowned upon by society—outside the cultural norm

The federal definition [established in IDEA (Individuals with Disabilities Education Act)] also includes a number of other features, ones that affect the individual's functioning in specified ways:

- An inability to learn that cannot be explained by intellectual, sensory, or health factors
- An inability to build and maintain satisfactory relationships with peers and teachers
- Inappropriate types of behavior or feelings under normal circumstances
- A general pervasive mood of unhappiness or depression

- A tendency to develop physical symptoms or fears associated with personal or school problems (5)

Other definitions emphasize that the condition being exhibited must be observed in *two different settings* (at least one being school-related)—and the condition is not responsive to general education interventions. A purpose of this school-related definition (two sources needed) is to eliminate the source of difficulty that is a result of a teacher-student relationship, for example, or simply *poor teaching*. In such cases the problem is not inherent to the student, who might be able to function well in other settings. A classification of EBD would then be inappropriate.

What *is* generally accepted is that the problem comes not just from the student or just the environment, but the interplay of both. For teachers it would be beneficial to focus not only on the student, but also on the social and academic environments (including the teacher himself) to get the best results.

There are two basic dimensions of behavioral disorder. They are referred to as *internalizing* and *externalizing*.

Externalizing involves striking out against others, often associated with conduct disorder. Blame goes outward as well. "Out there is the cause of my trouble." These individuals are represented in special education far more often than the internalizing group. The actions of this group are highly visible and often disturbing to a classroom or to particular students or adults.

Internalizing involves internal emotional or mental struggles, and might display as withdrawal, depression, or anxiety. Blame goes inward. Often these students can go unnoticed and therefore don't get the help or attention they might need. Although the externalizing student might create more trouble in school, the greater danger can be for the internalizing student as he sinks into depression or anger aimed toward himself.

Co-morbidity refers to the occurrence of two conditions at the same time—in this case the simultaneous co-occurrence of externalizing and internalizing conditions.

Anger is a common problem for EBD students. Anger while in school might result from an inability to perform as well as peers, from having to follow a full day of rules that are highly challenging, or from the difficulty of establishing satisfying social relationships. There are many opportunities throughout the course of a school day for irritations to mushroom into anger.

For the externalizing student, anger might lead to the disruption of classrooms and danger to other students. Anger can quickly jump to an extreme level and appear far out of proportion to the current situation. The control of anger is something that can be out of reach for many of these students at times, leading to trouble at school or with the law, as they strike out at others.

Anger for the internalizing student, usually directed at oneself, can lead to serious situations where self-worth is doubted and hope is abandoned. It is critical that teachers keep on the lookout for conditions such as this, and to get help before anyone gets hurt.

Addressing the needs of angry students is not an easy task. Students often become isolated due to hostility and aggression, and this only makes things worse. Students who are frequently irritating often alienate others, drawing negative attention to themselves. In turn, this creates more irritation for the student, and the spiral grows accordingly. Finding a way to interrupt this expanding spiral of anger at some point is essential.

Looking through a hundred "how to" articles regarding anger online or in books, you will not likely find one that suggests responding to student anger with anger as an effective management tool. In many cases it is exactly what the student is looking for. It is a success for her/him but a loss for the teacher. It can backfire for the teacher, making the situation worse.

Determining the triggers and results for these students can be very effective. What is it that sets them off? What rewards do they receive for their behaviors? What sustains it? We spoke in the prior section of this chapter about ABC (Antecedent-Behavior-Consequence) practice. This is a method that can have significant success with many of these students.

When setting up a behavioral chart to help manage behavior for (or with) these students, several questions might be considered: "How much can the student be brought into her own behavioral management program?" "How much can she accept that management is a good thing?" "How well can she separate herself from the behaviors she exhibits and understand that the *person* is accepted while the *behavior* is not?" "How effective can this intervention be?" The answers to such questions will help to guide the creation of the behavioral approach, and determine the participation level of the student herself.

Yet, we need not wait for a formal plan in order to begin our support. This can begin immediately. Building a personal relationship with these students is essential to their success in school and their functioning outside of school as well. Many different teachers, with widely varying teaching styles, can be effective with these students. Let's look at some general principles that are of value here.

One of the most important things for teachers to understand with these students is that when respect is given to the student it cannot necessarily be expected in return. In fact we might receive the opposite. This can be most difficult for a teacher (or parent). Remember—*you are not the target*. (See the book with this title by Laura Archera Huxley.) (6). It may seem that these students are intelligent and should know how their behavior affects others. While this might be true on some level, the behaviors are generally not there by choice.

I have worked with students, angry students, who would not have succeeded in the GED (General Educational Development) program they were in, for example, if I was to reflect the behavior or attitude they sent my way.

E.G. — EDMUND

In one case I recall being a young man's only remaining advocate in the program. Other teachers had expended their patience. I was able to keep Edmund from being expelled, as others wanted, yet he showed no appreciation and wouldn't even respond when I said hello to him in the morning. At times he just turned his back on me. What might have come out as an immediate reaction from me to his unpleasant behavior was tempered by my observation of the situation. I acknowledged to myself the various aspects of the interaction. I was able to experience sympathy and compassion on top of the flash of dark emotional reaction within. I learned to address the person, not the behavior, and was able to direct my own actions as a result (although I definitely addressed particular behaviors directly when needed—sternly at times). I also knew that Edmund was not capable of being his own advocate at this point, so I took on the role. In the end he left my presence with some level of success, a GED diploma. Without at least that much, his opportunity for success outside of school would be greatly diminished. There would be, I knew, plenty of opportunity for him to learn other life-lessons. They did not all need to come from our program.

I wish to note that there were, as well, students grappling with behavioral issues who were highly appreciative of the staff support. Not all were disrespectful. Considerable variation exists within this population.

My advocating or supporting students also did not always look the same. There were times when I sent students out of the classroom or out of the program because of their behavior. I made it very clear to them that the welfare of the class and learning environment were my first charges and that, if they interfered, I would not allow a disruptive student to remain in the classroom. They did learn, in general and in specific, that there were lines set that they could not cross without consequence.

Though the responses coming from me were tailored to the specific event at a particular moment, there existed an overlay of what would be considered out-of-bounds behavior. Behaviors such as open disrespect, name-calling, or endangering another would draw quick and strong reaction from me. And these responses needed to be consistent and persistent.

Sometimes a firm approach is what is most needed, and a shock is the best lesson. At other times, a bit of slack in a situation or appreciation by the teacher could go a long way toward developing trust between student and teacher and trust for the student within herself. But the whole picture needs to be studied. Some students, for example, might benefit most from a rigidly consistent approach to discipline and consequence, while other students don't need this and might even display more reactionary behavior because of it. Determine this ahead of time, ahead of problem interactions, as much as possible.

When considering an EBD classification there is an effort to distinguish between someone with a true disabling condition and someone who might be considered socially maladjusted (see below).

Social Maladjustment has not been defined by federal law so various individuals, organizations, and agencies use their own working definitions. One thing that is generally agreed upon, however, is that the exhibited behaviors have some measure of being willful, planned, or within the control of the individual. This does not warrant a special education classification.

The effects of EBD may be triggered or created by a wide variety of stimuli. For example, some EBD students have been affected by FAS (Fetal Alcohol Syndrome) or suffered *in utero* from smoke or other toxins. This is about physical and chemical damage. Physiological, psychological or other damage after birth can lead to problems just as severe.

TWO RECOMMENDATIONS FOR WORKING WITH THIS POPULATION

1. Seek multiple perspectives on students, behaviors, and situations related to the EBD condition. Most of a teacher's work will be solo in the classroom, but a wealth of value can come from the eye of another, a person who is not directly involved yet has appropriate knowledge and understanding of the condition and particular situation. Assembling a team of professionals and involved personnel on a regular basis would be the most valuable approach to take.

2. Understand what to expect in terms of respect. I have seen many teachers simply not have the ability to hold the care these

students needed. A student's lack of respect for them as a person and a teacher was just too big an issue. Yet, without someone to help, the outlook is bleak for the EBD student. I've been in many settings where these students have made considerable progress and learned to take better care of themselves. I know it can be done. Teachers can make a tremendous difference, and so can other adults in the student's life.

BOYS:

Boys far outnumber girls in the field of classified EBD—the official term for this is *disproportionate*. Inconsistent messages to boys regarding emotions—what is or isn't acceptable or appropriate and lack of avenues for understanding themselves—makes this an emotional rocky road.

Two male psychologists, Dan Kindlon and Michael Thompson, published a book called *Raising Cain: Protecting the Emotional Life of Boys*, which came out just twelve days before the Columbine High School shooting. (7) In it they speak of "emotional literacy" and the weakness of this for so many boys. They speak of aggression used as a defense mechanism, of the mixed messages given to boys regarding emotions, and the lack of understanding boys have of their inner world. All of this contributes to trouble and confusion for nearly half of the school-age population not to mention the male adults involved in various aspects of schooling.

Boys are emotional beings—just as girls are emotional beings. They are equally in need of the same basic nurturing qualities. By denying or ignoring these needs and not preparing boys for a rich, healthy, emotional life—we handicap them in their pursuit of a rich family life; an appropriate, rewarding career; and vibrant, personal fullness. Though there may be years of difficult learning to overcome, there still remains much that a teacher can do to help boys in this area. Understanding the general landscape and growing an awareness of how boys can be helped is a good place to begin.

EARLY EDUCATION:

Early education, before schooling even begins, can be one of the surest ways to interrupt a student's track toward EBD. Success at school socially, academically, and personally might eliminate much of the growing trouble for these students. "Early education and nurturing is absolutely critical... Children whose needs are met at an early age are able to go to school ready to learn...They're much less likely to be discipline problems in the classroom." (Oleta Garrett Fitzgerald, director of the Children's Defense Fund's Southern Regional Office.) (8) "Young people who generally end up in trouble were not prepared from the beginning educationally," Fitzgerald adds.

I leave you with this excerpt from Hallahan et al.:

> "Students with emotional or behavioral disorders typically have low grades... higher drop-out rates and lower graduation rates than other student groups, and are often placed in highly restrictive settings. Moreover, these students are disproportionately from poor and ethnic minority families and frequently encounter the juvenile justice system. Consequently, their successful education is among the most important and challenging tasks facing special education today." (9)

EXERCISE 18:
Support List

See section above entitled: **"Giving Students an Out."**

Create your list. Attempt to begin with three or five solid sources of support for students. Leave room for notes that you can add over time, indicating details such as:
- The support individual's basic info such as contact, available times, etc.
- The particular type of service available (both by title and by experience)

- What personality types might best benefit in this setting
- Things to watch out for or to prep students about
- Suggestions or requests that might be made of the service provider
- Complications that could occur such as with administration or particular agencies

ADHD (ATTENTION DEFICIT HYPERACTIVE DISORDER)

The terminology describing this group of individuals has changed many times since the first recorded example of a description of a hyperactive young man called Fidgety Phil in a poem by Heinrich Hoffman in 1865. ADHD individuals have been referred to as having "defective moral control," "minimal brain-damage," and more. While these descriptions have been abandoned, others have taken their place. Until recently this category was referred to as ADD, with or without Hyperactivity. The DSM-5 (Diagnostic and Statistical Manual of Mental Disorders, Fifth Edition) officially calls it ADHD, and divides it into three groups:

1. ADHD, Predominantly Inattentive Type
2. ADHD, Predominantly Hyperactive-Impulsive Type
3. ADHD, Combined Type (This third category combines both of the first two categories.)

A number of factors are considered strong possibilities for contributing to this condition, including heredity factors as well as toxins and medical factors. Also, the neurotransmitters *dopamine* and *norepinephrine* are often found in abnormal levels in individuals with ADHD. Neurotransmitters are chemicals that facilitate the transmission of messages between neurons in the brain. This can affect the processing of information, among other things.

Currently it is believed that one of the primary contributors to both the inattentive and impulsive aspects of ADHD is a problem with

behavioral inhibition. Russell Barkley's model of behavioral inhibition includes the ability to:
1. delay a response
2. interrupt an ongoing response if one decides that the response is inappropriate because of sudden changes in the demands of the task
3. protect a response from distracting or competing stimuli (10)

Behavioral inhibition allows time for *executive functions* to take place. This process can be interrupted or delayed in individuals with ADHD. Executive functions allow the individual to self-regulate behavior and to direct his own thoughts and actions. Barkley presents four general ways that ADHD individuals can exhibit problems with executive function.
1. Problems with WM (Working Memory) – indicating the ability to keep in mind what has been learned earlier and bringing that information into play in the current moment
2. Delayed Inner Speech – That inner "voice" that allows individuals to talk to themselves and decide how to proceed in any given moment
3. Difficulty controlling their emotions and their arousal levels – possibly with strong outbursts of joy or anger for example
4. Difficulty analyzing problems and communicating solutions to others (11)

Developing and maintaining long-term goals is another area of difficulty for individuals with ADHD. Without this the person is limited to moving from one thing to the next without *a thread to hold it all together*, without the benefit of progressing toward a goal. This limits the long-term outcome of efforts that are made and can directly affect success in school and in the workplace, resulting in lower academic achievement and poorer job-related performance.

They might also have problems with:
- Being organized—resulting in losing things, losing track of things, losing one's place in a process
- Feeling overwhelmed

- Feeling emotions strongly—accompanied by wide mood swings that can be difficult to manage
- Being on edge—not taking much to set themselves off
- Impulse control—reacting to things without enough thought, getting into trouble or saying things they later regret
- Having unusual sleeping patterns leading to difficulty following regular schedules
- Socializing with peers
- Being vulnerable to early drug use
- Coexisting conditions such as LD (Learning Disabilities), EBD, or substance abuse

From all of this we're able to see the elevated likelihood that students and others with ADHD bump up against many frustrations which can then lead to strong reactions such as anger. The extent of the inner challenges can lead directly to outer challenges which then compound the inner difficulties—an example of *downward spiral*.

What can we, as teachers, do to help these students to find success in school and in their lives, and decrease frustration and anger? We look at a selection:

CREATE EXTERNAL SPACE

Some of the anger in these students comes from feeling "penned-in," not fitting into aspects of the classroom scene, yet being forced to endure. Alleviation of this at critical moments is of great value to the student (and the entire classroom).

Locate areas in the school where the student can be sent to "run an errand," bring a note, make an inquiry, etc.

Create in-class space for pressure release. Recall the story of Daniel in Chapter Four who had difficulty sitting in a chair for longer than twenty minutes. The simple solution used worked wonders.

Identify a "safe space" where the student can move to when she notices anger starting to rise. The teacher and student together can set up the conditions for the use of this space. Yet ultimately, the student should monitor the need for this space herself. (See the story about Brad, earlier in this chapter, *Giving Students an Out*.

CREATE INNER SPACE

Help students develop a sense of "wait"—before speaking or acting, allowing a moment to reflect and view what is about to erupt. Advise the student to take these steps:

1. Notice any anger or other strong feelings stirring.
2. Immediately register a warning to yourself.
3. Pause briefly and consider using a less than *full-blast* word or action.

And consider these more advanced perspectives and actions:

4. Notice how the other party responds to you. Register this consciously.
5. Notice any changes or trouble spots in yourself.
6. Take control of yourself. Act as you wish to act, with deliberation rather than being driven by strong emotions that you *think* are who you are, while in reality may be intruders.

It will be advantageous for an individual to practice these steps during moments of low-level emotional charge. At the same time, practicing them during moments of high-level emotional charge might have the greatest impact and value. For teachers there is value in *first* being able themselves to practice as described above. Then the teacher can help students to do the same. The teacher will already have had firsthand experience with the struggle and the changes that can take place.

Another form of inner space for a student who gets angry, frightened, or anxious, might be to hold an image that for him can be calming and peaceful. It can be a place to visit in the imagination, or the image of inwardly visiting with a friend or favorite family member. The place might be real or not. The person might be alive or not. As a temporary action, the use of imagination at the appropriate moment can be a powerful tool.

CONNECT WITH STUDENTS

This broad subject might be approached in many ways. We consider a few:
- Develop trust (See Chapter Five)
- Take an interest in their interests
- Use humor
- Play (games, jokes, playful conversations and activities)
- Fair discipline
- Notice their areas of struggle and offer help or perspective
- Share goals that we, as teachers, are working on to improve our own lives and our teaching.

LET THEM EXPLORE

One of the beautiful aspects about many of these students is that they become interested in many things. Though it might be frustrating for a teacher or parent to see these blossoming interests quickly tossed aside for new interests, it may be best to just let it go. They'll keep exploring and learn about many things. Often these students will discover interests strong enough to stick with for long periods, or as central to a path of study or career.

When strong interests are piqued in the student, a teacher or parent might offer support and encouragement through books, tools, or experiences (such as a specialized camp). Overly supporting or encouraging can have a *backfire* effect, however, leading the student to react and resist. We might instead simply offer them the option of following their joy.

In school settings we might need to find creative ways to allow this to be. Yet, what could look unusual, such as a student with two assigned seats in the classroom, could in actuality promote a more smoothly operating class for all.

E.G. — GARY

One day my brother, Stephen, and I visited several artist shops/studios in a small Vermont town that was hosting an Artists'

Open House day. One gentleman, Gary, had a particularly impressive setup for his painting studio. Not only was it well lit, well supplied, and well tended, but adjacent to it was a wood shop where he built furniture and other things of beauty. Next to this room was a third studio—for making music. Gary was at the same time an instructor at Dartmouth College—and engaged in several other activities as well. The scope of it alone made Stephen and I feel tired.

As a child this artist was very active. "My feet never touched the ground," he told us. "But my parents were great. They gave me room to move and supplied me with all kinds of interesting things to engage with. I'm grateful to them."

There is a phrase that relates to this: *"to give a horse its head"* which means to allow a horse to gallop by lengthening the reins—to not hold it back. In this case it refers to letting a child explore and move as he is internally driven to move, so that he can learn about himself—his abilities, strengths, and limits. In this way the child can learn to make considerable contributions to family and society.

PHYSICAL EXERCISE

This is an important one. Exercise, movement, and strenuous activity can relieve much pent-up energy or anger. Physical activity can also help the student to have a clearer picture of himself and his environment by creating more balance within himself—both physical and emotional balance. It would be of significant value for the student to be able to recognize for himself when he is in need of physical action, even if he cannot immediately satisfy that need. He will better understand his needs and have a better chance at avoiding emotional overload and overreaction.

Someone to help coach the student's progress in this area would help—until the student's *inner-coach* could more efficiently monitor need and take action. Our goal as teachers then is to provide external support, leading toward more student self-guidance and independence, as it is in all areas of maturity and growth.

In specific, we can provide ample opportunity for physical movement and activity for the ADHD student. We can also encourage those students who are *not* drawn toward such physical activity to participate. And we must *not* take away recess or activity time as a punishment or discipline. Such actions usually make the entire situation worse, depriving the child from what is most needed.

WELCOME DIVERSITY

It's OK to be different. It's good to have difference in our students. Even difference that is bothersome or challenging at times, can be fruitful, productive—and, in the long run, rich. Various forms of diversity can lead to clearer and broader perspectives by all who are around it. Diversity is rich with potential for learning, understanding, and growth. Yet, while we might know this to be true, our actions don't always follow. One thing needed is intentional action. As teachers, we can improve our acceptance and support of students with ADHD by making a determined effort to do so.

The emphasis here is on the perspective of the teacher. It is the teacher who will facilitate the atmosphere that exists in the classroom and the development of acceptance.

Robin Williams, quite familiar with ADHD, spoke of the human condition and the preciousness of diversity: "You're only given a little spark of madness. You mustn't lose it." He was able to channel excess energy into actions that brought joy to many people for many years.

DEVELOP A VOCABULARY AROUND EMOTIONS

A vocabulary about emotions and one's emotional life is a very important tool for ADHD students. This is often an underdeveloped area in children, and especially boys. Without this there is little avenue available for these students to understand their emotions, to talk about them, or to relieve the weights and burdens that afflict them due to their emotional lives. Alienation from emotional language and knowledge can make a child feel like he is literally holding something alien within. The simple lack of communication around our emotional lives may make it all seem taboo or wrong to explore.

EMPHASIZE THE POSITIVE

Be happy with what you have. What a radical statement, in a day and age where consuming the new, the flashy, the media-determined "finest" and "next best" is drilled into us at every turn. Witness how toddlers are able to recognize a great many business logos far before they can read. Merchandising and marketing are reaching ever-younger populations. We are hit with the messages of "*more* is needed for me to be happy" from the moment we see the first advertisement on TV, or listen to radio, or ride an elementary school bus. Don't be satisfied with what you have—for it immediately turns old and must be replaced.

But we *can* look for the positive in what we have right now. We can continue to strive for more and at the same time appreciate *where we are* and *who we are* at the moment. As teachers practice this with themselves and their students, great things can happen. Appreciation in the moment can lead to satisfaction and self-appreciation which can then lead to increased school success and an overall improvement in a student's morale. This then leads to fewer angry outbursts and less conflict in school. We as teachers can be the model.

Finding satisfaction in our place and in ourselves is something that can benefit each of us. Studies show that a person who feels happiness will benefit in many ways, including enjoying better health, success at their work, and better relationships with spouse and friends. Common sense tells us the same thing. And there *is* much to be grateful for, even with difficulties that abound.

SELF-OBSERVATION AND SELF-AWARENESS
ACTIVITIES—**MINDFULNESS**

This is a reference that can be found repeatedly throughout this book. It is difficult to overstate the value of self-awareness in students who must, for their very survival, understand and manage themselves when they lose control. I have noticed that many students with classification seem to have a more mature sense of self-awareness than their peers. They must use this skill daily.

The growth of self-awareness is a process that extends throughout their school years and beyond. Many individuals in all walks of life dedicate their lives to better understanding themselves, whether they have special needs or not. (See Chapter Seven for more on Mindfulness.)

OTHER SPECIAL EDUCATION AREAS:

Many areas of special education, in addition to the three described above, will be regularly touched by anger in numerous ways. It often goes with the territory (though general education is by no means exempt). Some angry reactions may be shared across the board for several classifications, such as simply realizing that you have a classification and that you are viewed as *outside the norm*.

Other characteristics will differ between conditions such as TBI (Traumatic Brain Injury), OCD (Obsessive Compulsive Disorder), LD (Learning Disabilities), or Bipolar Disorder. Considerable information is available on each of the many diagnoses and classifications related to education and learning, though none of the bodies of information are complete. There is room for more professional study and room for deeper study on the part of each teacher, and each individual.

END-OF-CHAPTER QUESTIONS:

1. Can you recall an example of a conflict (though you may not have realized it at the time) between the concept and approach of "fair" versus "equal"? Do you feel that it is okay to treat students differently, even when it is obvious to other students? When might it *not* be okay?
2. Should special-ed students be taught alongside general-ed students? Included in the same classroom? What might be the upside and downside aspects of this practice? Which should prevail?
3. Consider five scenarios where students with exceptional needs might find difficulty in school, where tension might build up. What might be some potential solutions or outlets for this tension? What reasonable tactics might the students employ?
4. Have you experienced disrespect from a student? How much control do you feel the student had over him/herself? Would your reaction to the behavior be different if it seemed that the behavior was the result of a special need, an ingrained learned behavior, or a lazy effort to be civil?
5. Would your response to the different behaviors in question four be automatic—depending on your perception of the interaction, or your mood at the time, or a deliberate action on your part?
6. In what ways do you, as a parent or teacher, let off steam when tension builds? Can you do this at a moment of crisis or only later, after time has passed?
7. In what ways have you had conversations with students about an inner, emotional environment? What has been the response of the students? Has it differed for boys and girls in regard to maturity, verbal fluency, and/or willingness to engage?
8. What new practices can you bring to your classroom or home regarding these topics?

CHAPTER SEVEN

THE INNER APPROACH

"Compassionate listening is to help the other side suffer less. If we realize that other people are the same people as we are, we are no longer angry at them."
—Thich Nhat Hanh

WHAT IS MEANT BY THE INNER APPROACH?

Inner approach here refers to the practice of intentionally studying and maturing the understanding we have of ourselves—the way we function and the ability we have to affect how we function. Another aspect of an inner approach to growth, in addition to the effort to understand, is the ability to *experience* in new ways and with new depths.

In regards to anger, the effort is to reach the roots and triggers of this strong emotion before they manifest in behaviors which can be troublesome for the individual or others. A clear picture of one's own functioning in relation to anger will allow this to happen. This effort does not equate with practices such as psychoanalysis or uncovering the deep *why* of our behaviors or tendencies. The goal is to accurately observe our current functioning and to be able to influence it going forward.

A clear view of oneself may be an elusive target. Even the acceptance that there is value in "going deeper" into self-study is often questioned—or simply ignored. Those who see the value have opportunities before them.

Several practices may be found that are focused on this type of growth. Some are aligned more with an intellectual approach, some more with the heart, some both. We consider in this chapter a selection of well-established practices. There exist many others, some of considerable value, some not.

One other point is worth making before we proceed. There is a natural growth that occurs in human beings, even as toddlers grow to be walkers, that mirrors this drive for self-investigation and discovery. In the beginning it is a natural process, inherent in the progression of maturing. Then, as we age, the process often withers through lack of intention and will to see more. Perhaps it is the effect of an uninterested society, or a lack of practice and instruction in how to proceed, that leaves us without interest and capacity to maintain an inner search. But something more is needed as we mature, to help turn that natural drive we have as babies and children into intentional self-study.

The excitement and deep satisfaction that can be experienced through inner exploration may still be alive at a later age, and even be amplified as we become acutely aware of the growth and possibilities before us. Yet, this will not happen on its own. Effort and attention are needed. We may look for teachers and fields of inquiry that resonate with us to help us along the way (a sampling is listed below). We can watch for the pitfalls of relying too much on teachers and programs. We can aim to strengthen our inner drive and inner understanding—and as we do, we can pass this process, this inner strength, on to our students.

PRE-OCCUPIED:

Sounding quiet and benign, the term *preoccupied* is often used without much consideration of its actual meaning. To be preoccupied means that as we enter new moments, new situations—something is already in place occupying our attention—leaving less room for new seeing, thinking, or experiencing. Something is occupying our thoughts, our feelings, our ability to perceive and assess with depth or clarity. There is a dullness.

Being pre-occupied happens not only during day-dreaming or obsessing. To a mild degree it happens nearly constantly in each of us, most always "below the radar". The goal of an inner approach to improving as a teacher is based on the ability to lighten up the continuously streaming preoccupation. Whether we are aware or not of this preoccupation, inner growth can lighten its effect on us. The result is vital and vibrant.

EXERCISE 19:
Pre-occupy

> Are you preoccupied? How can you tell at any particular moment? To make an attempt, choose set times or circumstances to observe your thoughts—to simply see where they are. This is a particularly elusive task, for as soon as we make any attempt to see we suddenly are seeing. We are awake to the moment, and any preoccupied thoughts are instantly banished. At this point it will seem as if there were no times when our thoughts or attention drifted from the present moment.
>
> Yet, with practice, we might begin to notice a variety of things.
> 1. We notice more of what was occupying our thoughts at the interval moment we set.
> 2. We begin to see a pattern or repetition of circling thoughts—or thoughts associated with the specific activity—our personal repertoire.

3. We naturally develop an increased awareness of when our thoughts are miles away from where our body is.

Regarding the moments or intervals to observe, options might be to:
- use a phone-timer (not in the classroom, unless there is an activity for all members of the class to engage in using the timer)
- notice each time you open your mouth to speak
- notice this as often as possible (whenever you think of it), for a set half-hour period, then let it go and set up another half-hour period at another time

INNER PRACTICES: A SELECTION OF CONTEMPORARY AND TRADITIONAL APPROACHES

MINDFULNESS

The term mindfulness has been around for a many years, yet in the 21st century it has seen increasing usage and popularity. The term itself can cover a gamut of meaning and, as the following definitions portray, a range in depth; from a simple quality of *being aware of something*, to *a heightened state of being*.

Definition—Oxford English Dictionary (OED):
mindfulness: The quality or state of being conscious or aware of something: "their mindfulness of the wider cinematic tradition"; *a mental state achieved by focusing one's awareness on the present moment, while calmly acknowledging and accepting one's feelings, thoughts, and bodily sensations, used as a therapeutic technique.*(1)

Increasingly, the practice of mindfulness is being brought into schools for the benefit of both student and teacher. The benefits mindfulness can have with anger reduction are well noted in books and articles—both with the lessening of anger that is hot in the moment, and as a preventative measure. As students learn how to more fully focus on anger and its triggers in themselves, for example, the more able they are to prevent eruptions of anger. In addition, as individuals learn to be more fully awake to each moment of their experience, the less likely it will be that anger will jump into action. It loses volatility.

"In a culture of constant technological stimulation, it's important to teach kids the power of mindfulness. And, with teenagers being the most stressed group of people in the United States when school is in session, learning stress-management techniques is essential," says Dana Santas of CNN. "A high school in Marblehead, Massachusetts is seeing the benefits of a mindfulness meditation initiative that began last year, with many students reporting feeling less anxious and more relaxed." (2)

Mindfulness practices are often especially important for students with challenging conditions such as ASD, EBD, ADHD, and others (see Chapter Six, Classified), where anger is often quick to surface and difficult to manage. Out of necessity these students become aware of how they function and how to have some control over this, or suffer the results. They must learn and practice continually a level of mindfulness that is right for them. Mindfulness is not something that is learned once and then is over. The efforts must be continually renewed so that the awareness and abilities stay fresh.

One popular trend in mindfulness is the *Vipassana* movement. Vipassana, which began in Burma in the 1950s, has gained much popularity in the United States over past decades. This is an ancient Buddhist meditation technique, now explored and practiced by people from all walks of life. The essential meaning of Vipassana is *to see things as they are*.

METACOGNITION

Definition—Oxford English Dictionary (OED):
metacognition: *Awareness and understanding of one's own thought processes.* (3)

Definition—Dictionary.com:
metacognition: Higher-order thinking that enables understanding, analysis, and control of one's cognitive processes, especially when engaged in learning. (4)

Metacognition means cognition about cognition, or knowing about knowing. We observe how we function and bring awareness to our higher-order thinking skills. Many benefits arise from this effort, including for school children. Rae Jacobson tells us, "Reflecting on our own thoughts is how we gain insight into our feelings, needs, and behaviors — and how we learn, manage, and adapt to new experiences, challenges, and emotional setbacks. It's the running conversation we have in our heads, mentally sounding ourselves out and making plans. Training kids to use it proactively to overcome obstacles, it turns out, can be a powerful tool." (5)

Many of the problems children face in schools, including around anger and other strong emotions, might be approached with increased strength and efficiency, with an increase in metacognitive abilities. "Metacognitive thinking teaches us about ourselves," says Tamara Rosier. "Thinking about our thinking creates perspective—perspective that leaves room for change." She gives an example: "Instead of saying, 'Math tests make me anxious,' we're asking ourselves, 'What is it about math tests that makes me feel anxious and what can I do to change that?' " (6)

We constantly talk to ourselves when we are awake, except perhaps for moments when we can successfully quiet our minds through levels of meditation. Having some influence over the continuous conversations in our minds can provide us a measure of freedom from thoughts and feelings that weaken us or take us in directions we do not intend or desire.

Students who are faced with learning or behavioral challenges may benefit greatly from metacognitive skills. Not only can this help with their study habits, but also with behavioral control and self-regulation of various forms. Self-study and self-regulation have been at the forefront of useful skills for these students. (See Chapter Two for more on inner voice.)

TEACH EMPATHY

Definition—Oxford English Dictionary (OED):
empathy: The ability to understand and share the feelings of another; awareness and understanding of one's own thought processes. (7)

Definition—Dictionary.com:
empathy: The psychological identification with or vicarious experiencing of the feelings, thoughts, or attitudes of another. (8)

When so much attention is focused in society today on what *I* want and what *I* need, it's heartening to see the growing trend toward discussing and investigating *empathy*. With this, we turn our focus on comprehending the perspective of others rather than dwelling on or mindlessly following our personal interests and desires. This practice allows an individual a first step toward broadening vision and deepening experience, once the constriction of *me-me-me* is weakened.

Students in varied settings are being exposed to the value of empathy, and in many cases attempts are being made to deepen the student's experience with this. Questions remain, however, about how best to teach empathy, or whether it *can* even be taught at all.

The approach of the teacher in a classroom will determine whether words spoken can be heard with any depth. The emotional and psychological state of the teacher will determine whether students can feel in themselves what empathy is about, and thus be able to take a deeper step into another person's feelings and perspective.

Teaching empathy is not something to be taught outside of oneself. If I as a teacher cannot or am not residing in a condition of empathy, then I have no right to teach it to others. It becomes an empty thing in this way, like teaching ancient history from writings based on other writings from prior writings. Yes, something might transmit through all of this, but not with the vibrancy of looking into what is unfolding in the moment—what is felt, sensed, understood—experienced intimately.

Empathy is something that a child begins learning from birth. But it is not guaranteed. According to Gwen Dewar, PhD, "Empathy isn't something you either have or lack, and it isn't something that develops automatically, without input from the environment." (9) The way that parents, teachers, and others communicate and share with babies, children, and young adults will help determine their ability to empathize with others. Again, Gwen Dewar: "Babies thrive when their parents assume they have minds of their own, and take the time to figure out what their babies are thinking and feeling. In particular, children seem to benefit when they have ...parents who communicate *accurately* about mental and emotional states." (10)

By the time children reach school age much has been established regarding the capacity for empathy in each of them. Yet the potential for growth does not end here. Much can yet be learned and experienced. In general, teaching empathy is not an easy thing to do and distinct efforts must be made in order to have success. "Empathy is a complex concept and a difficult skill. It's time for educators to recognize the strength it takes to create, balance, and sustain an empathic mindset in a culture that doesn't always value it." Brianna Crowley and Barry Saide. (11)

Yet, empathy might also be transmitted in significant ways through more simple routes, such as through acting as a role-model (if we can call this simple). Again, we see the substantial value at play with a teacher's feelings and behaviors. Modeling empathy and being caring with students is the first line of effort in this arena, the first line of learning about empathy and how to practice it, consciously or not.

E.G. — JASON

Jason was asked to visit a classroom to help with a growing friction that was manifesting between the fifth-grade students there. He set up a series of four *mindfulness* classes for the group, beginning with simple exercises to help students quietly notice their breathing and sensing. Some of the effects of such exercise were immediate in the tone and pace of the participants, even on this simplest of levels. In a session soon after, Jason led them through an exercise called *Good Will and Good Wishes*, where everyone focuses their attention on a specific person or group of people such as our mother, our parents, or those who are hungry. This day, when the students appeared inwardly and outwardly quiet, he led them through the focusing of good will and good wishes on one of the students in the class—then on another—and on again until all shared the experience. Each person got to focus on each other, and each student experienced being the sole focus of attention by the group. The change in the class was profound. A level of empathy and care was being opened for each member of the class, with no criticism and no mention of *empathy* or *change* at all. An opening was created, an acceptance was experienced.

The gap between approaches to the teaching of empathy is inherent in the vocabulary itself. Are we attempting a teaching of empathy or a transmission of empathy? Is this something students learn primarily with the mind or something experienced more thoroughly? "Is empathy a skill that can even be taught? A 'competency' you should bullet point in your lesson plan and pre-assess for? Or is it something more full and persistent and whole?" asks Terry Heick. He continues with this. "Students would learn to empathize rather than be taught to empathize, as a symptom of what they know." (12)

Another area of concern lies in the question, what do we do with our newly enhanced abilities? Feeling what another feels, seeing as another sees, can be a weight to carry, both in being inside another and seeing yourself from a new set of eyes. Hopefully, as we grow we will at the same time experience a willingness to be gentle with others and ourselves. This is something that can be broached by a teacher who feels comfortable doing so if the teacher has some personal experience to draw upon. This is an area of great importance and consequence. May minds and hearts be open and possibilities be explored.

E.G. — COLIN

Colin Ryan told a story on *The Moth Radio Hour, Saved by the Belle*, aired on WAMC radio on Friday, June 1, 2018. (13) He described a setting, in sixth grade, when he was being totally humiliated in front of his new class at the beginning of the school year. It arose simply from students offering some of their interests, in an effort to learn about each other and become more familiar. It wasn't working for Colin. He described the feeling that,"…one can either be cool or invisible." He wanted at that moment to be invisible. That also was not working. Students were snickering at the responses he gave—different from their own responses. As he became more and more embarrassed suddenly something surprising happened. A voice rang out from the back of the room. "Cut it out!" There was silence. Michelle Seaver, a cool girl in class had spoken. Others listened. Then she went on, turning to the teacher. "Why are you letting this happen? What is the point of this if we are just going to make fun of each other?" Colin said that he did not remember the name of the teacher or any student in class except for Michelle Seaver, remembering both her first and last name. He then realized that there was a third option to cool or invisible (neither of which leads to being remembered for long, or at all). The third option was, "If you stand up for somebody when they need you most, then you'll be remembered as their hero for the rest of their life."

It is hopeful that, in that moment, the teacher listened to what the brave student had to teach, and learned something of value.

YOGA

Many forms of yoga exist within this country alone, and far more outside of this. We often think of yoga as primarily a physical activity, with a level of relaxation mixed in. Yet many practitioners are able to observe the mental and emotional benefits of yoga practice as well, such as improved concentration and a feeling of peace.

In some traditions there are forms of yoga that focus specifically on different aspects of human growth. A Hindu tradition, for example, has three primary yoga approaches. Karma Yoga indicates the path of *Action*. Bhakti Yoga refers to the path of *Devotion*. Jnana Yoga is the path of *Knowledge*. Once again we can see, in these serious practices, the focus on physical, emotional, and mental aspects of personal growth. Any of these yoga approaches could engage a person's focus full-time for a lifetime.

With the wide selection of yoga practices available to each of us there exists the possibility of finding one that we feel well-suited for. From a mild yet effective Yin yoga, to a sweat-it-out hot yoga like Bikram, the choices might focus more on the physical or the spiritual, on exercise or meditation.

Benefitting from yoga practice holds true for younger individuals, both children and teens, as it does for adults. More and more schools are employing forms of yoga with students, both as a physical practice and as a calming practice.

Yoga In Schools (YIS) is a nonprofit organization that provides yoga programming and teacher training to several school districts in Pittsburgh, Pennsylvania. "Our mission is to empower students and teachers with yoga-inspired exercises to promote lifetime wellness. Our vision is to make yoga available in all schools so that students and teachers develop body-mind awareness and the ability to nurture their own wellbeing." (14) This is one of many organizations currently promoting yoga in schools.

Yoga as a physical activity can also create a more level playing-field for students of different abilities. "Yoga doesn't discriminate ....Whether an athlete or not, everyone is equally matched in their own bodies during a yoga practice, where the focus is internal." This can help students who usually feel marginalized or embarrassed in physical education classes to experience increased confidence and to better fit in. Less stress and anxiety is the result.

Yoga can specifically help some students who have *classified* challenges. "As a mother ... with a child who is on the autism spectrum, I can attest to the myriad benefits, ranging from physical advantages like improved sport performance and posture to profoundly valuable mental skills like self-control and the ability to manage stress....I developed this [breathing] exercise specifically for my son with Asperger's syndrome. It's very effective for children prone to panic attacks or tantrums." By Dana Santas, Special to CNN. (15)

Put simply, yoga helps prevent the build-up of stress and frustration that can lead to explosions of anger. "Self-regulatory coping skills and resilience are believed to be effective countermeasures for stress, which may lessen the development of mood and affect-related problems." And it can help one understand when and to what degree anger might be appropriate. "Gandhi found no problem with feeling anger, only with how it was expressed. 'I'm continually telling people, we don't get to be different people —but we do get to be wiser about how we put them [the same neuroses] out in the world.'" Alan Reder. (16)

Children stand to gain much understanding about their body and its connection to emotions through an experience with yoga. If we wait until they are out of school before exposing them to practices such as yoga, they will have lost years of potential gain, across a broad spectrum. A selection of benefits suggested in "Benefits of Yoga in Schools" (17) follows—

Mind:
- Relieves tension and stress
- Improves ability to be less reactive; more mindful of thoughts, words, and actions

Body:
- Develops core strength, essential for good posture and correct physical alignment

- Relaxes the body, promoting better sleep

Spirit:
- Supports character development and emotional intelligence
- Supports a sense of universal connectedness

We can see by listing only a few of the possible benefits from exposing children to yoga practice, how many of the goals set in this book can be more easily met. Anger will have far less of a stronghold in children who experience these individual and communal strengths.

The above list of inner practices is, as mentioned, partial. There are many forms of practice that could help students with focus, empathy, self-esteem, compassion, and more. Some of the forms such as the softer, more fluid martial arts like Aikido will promote physical benefits as well— including strength, balance, and proprioceptive awareness.

TRANSFORMATION:

Transformation is not a term often used in the field of education, but it is one that is hinted at repeatedly. Nearly every textbook covering the basics of education will refer to a teacher being aware of personal attributes such as cultural biases, voice, and teaching style. It will then be recommended that a teacher adapt where needed in order to be as fair, efficient, and effective as possible in working with a diverse population of students. A teacher is charged with change, both change in herself and change in her students. This is how a beginning teacher becomes a novice teacher, and eventually moves on to become a master teacher. Yet, the master teacher is still not perfected. If a teacher thinks he is perfected, then he has stopped learning and growing. Only when the teacher is able to keep alive that vibrancy that comes with learning something new, experiencing something deeper, or gaining expanded understanding can he grow and change and keep vitality in the teacher-student connection.

Change in this instance entails much more than changing the decoration in a classroom or even effecting change in the use of one's voice.

THE INNER APPROACH

Change here means transformation—change on a deep level, such as developing the ability to quickly perceive the essence or underlying influences at play in a conflict, or observing one's own inner state (as referred to in Chapters One, Two, and Four) when approaching a situation. One might then perceive differently, notice changes in one's feeling, or open to new ways of thinking.

The exercises, stories, and narratives found in this book are presented as both stimulus and guidepost for those who continually wish for more in their lives, more even than the accumulation of wealth, power, or prestige. We might, with effort, move beyond the limitations of our own character. This is profound transformation, as we give a bit of weight to the much bandied phrase, "a new me."

This description of transformation is considered by many to be the natural state of humans, separating us from other creatures of the earth—to know more about ourselves and to build the capacity to influence the direction a life can take. As Socrates so ably directed us, "Know thyself."

In the classroom, beyond learning new tricks, management tools, and strategies (all of which are important), transformation is about creating a significant change in the way a teacher can see and act. This change is more than tweaking a personality or changing behavior. It arises from an inner shift, a substantial change in the capacity of an individual to perceive and understand. It is as though the center of gravity in a person moves in a direction from outer to inner, where learning now occurs from the newfound vision and clarity. Reliance by the teacher begins to shift from books, workshops, and trainings to direct perception and insight. The very character of a person can morph and mature, allowing deeper and more immediate learning to take place. A new classroom experience comes to life.

At the same time, while learning to rely on our growing inner strength and vision, we might notice enriched sources of learning around us. We simultaneously rely more deeply on our individual effort as well as appropriate input from our environment.

To effect transformation is neither a shallow nor a partial matter. The complete person must be addressed. References have been made throughout this book regarding varied aspects of human growth and development such as physical, mental, and emotional growth. It is not for variety or creating choice that these basic elements of a life are presented. They are offered as indicators of arenas which may be intentionally studied and developed, and when developed together simultaneously, significant changes may occur—changes that are sought. As the saying goes, "The whole becomes more than the sum of its parts." Significantly more.

Let's consider one small example of the type of profound change we are speaking of. Picture a person you might know who you would describe as *reactionary*. The smallest thing can make him defensive (you sense a pulling back on your part, a loss of connection). If he perceives a slightly greater affront, he begins to bristle. From here the escalation in reaction can soar. Reactions might seem quite out of proportion to the situation at hand.

Then picture seeing this friend after a year of absence. He seems changed. No longer does he automatically throw up a defense at any perceived slight. No longer does he seem disturbed by others' opinions much at all, yet at the same time he feels connected, no longer distant. You would wonder what has happened to this friend of yours. What has led to such a great and deep change. This would be one example of personal transformation—far more than suppression of anger or anger-management— some measure of freedom.

Taking this a step further, imagine having an argument with a student in your class and recognizing your tone and actions. On one hand, you feel like yelling at this person, for she is making the same old argument based on completely wrong assumptions and disturbing you and the entire class—again. If this is the only scenario pictured by you, then you will act according to this information. On the other hand, you might recognize a cry for help, for real connection, and think that maybe there is something you can be doing to help her, rather than thinking to blame her. Your beginning reaction might be the same in each situation described, but the second action carries more depth of perception and the possibility of more thorough communication with the student.

THE INNER APPROACH

The difference in results can be dramatic. Most teachers with moderate experience can recognize those moments when feeling like they said just the right thing, or conversely, the wrong thing, at a particular moment. Knowing what to say is of immense value, and this comes not only from preparing ahead of time. Cultivating an able inner stance may provide the capacity we seek.

It may be easy to see that our "friend" above, who changed so deeply, has experienced a level of freedom, freedom from certain grips on his thoughts, feelings, and actions. Freedom and transformation are closely linked. (To read more about "Freedom" please see Chapter Nine.)

Communication and perception at the level we are speaking of here will have an effect considerably wider than that between two individuals. The society of the classroom as well as the greater community will be affected. John Bennett puts it into an even larger perspective. "The very aim of society seems to be to remove from people responsibility for their lives and acts. The way of transformation must be the exact opposite of this. Whatever else it might lead to, it must make us into free, responsible individuals, able to direct our own lives in accordance with the greatest objective good." (18)

END-OF-CHAPTER QUESTIONS:

1. What is one particular inner approach that you have experience with? How has it affected your personal life?
2. Has there been discussion or reference made to one's emotional life in your classroom or in your interaction with children and youth? In what context? To what purpose?
3. Has there been direct discussion of *inner-life* with this same population—of growth and change that is beyond academics and the intellectual?
4. Have any of the specific techniques referred to in this chapter been employed in your classroom or home? To what effect?

5. How might your students benefit from the practices presented in this chapter? Is there a specific need for this right now? What specifically can you do to implement into your classroom or your life one or more of the approaches discussed within? Envision clearly, describe.
6. How might it be possible to reach levels of understanding or depths of experience that are currently beyond our ability to see, to even comprehend? How might we move toward this?
7. Can you recall teachers in your own history of schooling who have helped you with inner exploration (social, emotional, spiritual, personal transformation)? Was it more implicit or explicit?
8. Is the effort of transformation something that holds your attention? Outer transformation—"What would you like to be when you grow up?" Inner transformation—"I will strive to be a good listener" or "I wish to find my purpose." (Though, of course, there is considerable overlap.)

CHAPTER EIGHT

THE TEACHER I.E.P.

"The best fighter is never angry."
—**Lao Tzu**

PRACTICE

Setting a practice for oneself with times and targets will offer the discipline and development needed for the growth of a serious teacher. The following practice, the *Teacher IEP*, presents varied forms of exercise and approach to the multifaceted expansion which each teacher might enjoy.

A substantial exercise for a teacher who wishes to enhance her classroom experience and ability is called the *Teacher IEP*. The term IEP (Individualized Education Plan) officially refers to an instrument that is used to identify and support students who are referred to as *exceptional learners* (See chapter six for more on exceptional learners.) The term IEP was written into law in 1990 in the legislation called IDEA (Individuals with Disabilities Education Act), which grew out of the early important federal law known as P.L. 94-142 or the "Education for All Handicapped Children Act" passed in 1975.

The IEP is the backbone of the special education process, ensuring that every student (including students with different learning, receptive, and expressive needs) receives the support needed to have an equal chance at success in school. It is a written document that's used to track and measure the progress that a student makes, and to keep, drop, or adjust the educational program designed for him or her as needed for progress and success.

The Teacher IEP is similar in that it also is a written document used to track and measure progress in the educational arena. It differs in that it's written for teachers, not students, and it's not an official document. The teacher IEP (representing Intellectual–Emotional–Physical development) has been created by the author in order to facilitate teacher growth, including the ability to move through each teaching day with clear thinking, unclouded emotions, and a physical state of strength and endurance. It too is concerned with exceptional learning and with the development of human potential.

Each student, who is twenty-one years of age or younger who has been classified as having a "special need" related to education is entitled to an IEP (Individualized Educational Plan). The goals set down in these IEPs and the special programs designed for these students range from lofty to concrete. All are intended to bring out the best in each student in a variety of target areas. It is for this very reason that teachers also stand to benefit from an IEP, individually designed and geared toward bringing out the best in each. These particular IEPs will have some differences. They will be designed for teachers' needs, will be self-generated, and self-monitored. Yet, like the student IEP's, they might help support profound and valued change.

To help students to "...*realize their full human potential*" teachers must strive to realize their own full human potential. Through this practice they will be able to model the effort, and understand what is actually needed to make significant change. These are lofty goals indeed. As experienced teachers well know, the road toward lofty aims is paved by bricks of *concrete*—both short-term and long-term concrete goals.

THE TEACHER I.E.P.

I IS FOR INTELLECTUAL—

Every teacher goes through intellectual training to become a teacher and must pass certain hurdles designed to give an adequate measure of intellectual ability related to the specific educational field entered. This is an essential component of the teacher training process. A threshold is reached. Equally important is that a teacher does not stop learning at this point, or at any point along the way in her career. Much as a shark must swim or sink, so must a teacher continue to engage in the process of learning, or *she* will begin to sink. No longer will she bring to class the model of a lifelong learner. No longer may she move through the day with a spring in her step. No longer will she catch the many minute moments of learning that help a teacher assess and adjust her actions and deliver the best for her students.

Other aspects of intellectual development take place outside the "halls of education" where teacher training is offered. Mental strength in its myriad forms may be explored, and a wide range of knowledge and development might be appreciated.

What follows is a series of focus topics, in the form of questions that may help teachers explore some of these areas of intellectual knowledge and ability and develop their own individualized programs relating to the intellect.

- Is the physical brain getting what it needs for optimum performance (e.g., rest and nutrition)? Be specific! Investigate. Observe your own habits and practices.
- What thoughts do I invite in for conversation? Of the nearly constant parade of thoughts that we have running through our minds, which ones do we "invite for conversation"? These are the ones that determine where our attention goes and what our life becomes built around.
- What intellectual traits and strengths would I like my own child to have (e.g., the determination and ability to complete what is begun)?
- What does it mean to be "open-minded"?

- What do I do for intellectual play? What is the value of intellectual play? Examples?
- Am I able to use my intellectual ability as a tool? Can I separate my mind from my emotions and physical state when I need to be objective and not muddy my thinking? Can I even see that there are levels to mental clarity? Explain.
- What kinds of activities should I practice? What do I wish to emphasize? Hence, what targets do I set for myself intellectually? And what portion of my intellectual strivings is best kept loose, undirected, open to creativity?
- Should I find a teacher for myself? What do I wish to learn?
- What kind of person do I want to be?
- How can I strengthen the depth, duration, and focus of my attention?
- What are some of my strongest beliefs? How do they affect me—my teaching, my view of the world?
- How seriously am I able to listen to others who hold different beliefs?
- What other questions can I ask of myself regarding this amazing human tool of *intellect*?

E IS FOR EMOTIONAL—

This involves that part of us that brings color to an otherwise black, white, and gray world. Emotions also allow us to understand and empathize with others around us, to "step into their shoes." Emotions open us to experiences that can be had in no other way.

The range of emotions that we experience as a species or as an individual human is vast, especially when we look at other living species. Emotions penetrate all of our thoughts and actions in some way, at varying degrees. Emotions are not separate, yet they are—for our thoughts, emotions, and actions are all in play at every moment of our day, though sadly not cooperating or communicating with one another for the most part. Each of these aspects of us has its own agenda.

THE TEACHER I.E.P.

Consequently, some level of conflict and miscommunication is always present.

No matter how we interpret the purpose of our emotional lives, the value of emotional health cannot be ignored. It becomes all too clear when something goes wrong and we are drained of energy or led down difficult paths.

Emotional strength must at least provide teachers with an energy level equivalent to the fine emotional fuel burned each day in the classroom, and emotional strength is something that clearly can be developed. Whether we wish to benefit from more control over the words that leave our mouths, or to learn to use anger as a tool, or to learn new ways to energize ourselves—asking questions of ourselves can be a strong way to begin. Then might we "enter the ring" and grapple with that colorful, vibrant, volatile emotional world that helps make each of us who we are.

- What is the purpose of our emotions?
- What are my top five "buttons" that get pushed? Are *negative* buttons the ones that are automatically brought to mind? How might sentimentality, nostalgia, or joy fit in?
- How might I greet these "reactions" so that they do not control me?
- How might I increase my ability to see the "triggers" for these buttons before they grab me?
- How can I strengthen those moments that emotionally feed me throughout the day? Make a list. Explore.
- How do students see me as I behave in each moment, especially when not engaged in official teaching times?
- How do my emotions affect my thinking at any given moment?
- How do my thoughts and physical state affect my emotional state? How sensitive am I to their influence?
- Is there any way to protect myself from being dragged into useless or destructive emotions?
- Can I learn?
- How can I diminish my dependence on the energy of negative emotions?

- How can I feed an emotional life that delivers energy and joy?
- Is this what I really want?
- How can this emotional life help me connect more strongly to others?

P IS FOR PHYSICAL—

Being physically fit for teaching involves more than the ability to walk and talk, considerably more. The physical demand for a teacher in a classroom is constant, and if physical energy stores run out before the day is done, the emotional and intellectual concentration needed will plummet as well. A depleted teacher is of minimal use in the classroom, or worse.

The wellbeing of many individuals is at stake. A teacher who has the stamina to stay energized throughout the day may remain vital and poised, and keep her/his emotional and intellectual edge intact. We might even prepare for teaching as we would prepare for a marathon. Teaching does, in fact, feel like a grueling marathon at times, and we may need to push through "the wall."

There is more, as well, beyond physical strength and stamina at play in the classroom. A teacher who is attuned and poised physically may feel as though the activity of the classroom is like a dance. There is a flow and grace and joy that can be transferred to students, and a vibrant energy generated.

- Am I getting the "food" I need for proper physical development and maintenance? Could an even finer level of food produce a finer level of health and vigor?
- How can I create energy throughout the day while in the midst of teaching? Observe closely what currently works for you. What are the sources? They might be subtle, elusive. What can you add to your repertoire?
- Am I "running out of steam" before I run out of the teaching day?
- Do these shoes work for me all day long?

- Are the thoughts that pull me away draining my physical strength?
- Am I carrying emotional weights that affect me physically?
- Where do I hold tension in my body? How can I address this? Internally or with outside help?
- Do I try to tackle some problems physically that can be better addressed intellectually or emotionally?
- What "energy leaks" can I identify? Posture? Tension? Physical Habits? Energy leaks will include emotional and intellectual leaks as well, such as doubt, impatience, and negative emotions.

THE BEAUTY

The beauty of all of this coalesces when an effort is made in all three arenas simultaneously. What might become apparent to practitioners is that nearly all individuals favor one of these three development areas over the others. This primarily unconsciously chosen path determines how we see the world and interpret the bulk of the data that enters us. This is not necessarily a bad thing, just unbalanced. Relying on essentially only one of the three basic avenues of experiencing the world around us cuts us off from the awareness of so much more. It can also hold us to a shallow level of experience, compared to what is possible.

By concurrently developing the intellectual, emotional, and physical aspects of ourselves, we allow a synergy to form that creates openings to sources of energy that exist all around us. We can find intellectual stimulation working with students. We can experience moments of joy and washes of satisfaction. We can proceed with a light step, for the whole is far greater than the sum of its parts. A well-working machine can carry us easily through the day, where the students are the big winners.

It has been said that in the days of our intrepid foremothers and forefathers, those of rebellious spirits and practical action, that they "… set into the field with a plow in one hand and Descartes in the other…" These hardy individuals, who helped establish and develop this country, did not leave their intelligence at home when they entered the field to work. Nor did they leave their strength, stamina, or work ethic in the field when intellectual pursuits called. As much as they brought *all*—to each setting, to each moment of their lives—they experienced that synergistic strength of a team working closely together. And how much closer a team can there be than to blend the strengths of the three bodies that live within each of us: intellectual, emotional, and physical? Each is constantly active, whether working together or at odds. It is up to each of us to choose how they, and essentially we, function.

EXERCISE 20:
The Teacher IEP

Determine the amount of time you wish to set for the overall project. (Three weeks? One month?)

Divide the time into three blocks (time periods). A minimum of one week each is suggested.

Begin with the first of the three sections, and work with it for the first block.

Select three questions from that section, and spend some time with each:

- Consider how you function in that particular area (thinking back—thinking forward).
- Observe yourself in action, related to each topic. (It will take practice to do this well.)
- Write notes for yourself on all this. Do not wait until a later time to write it all down. Do not wait to do these exercises until the time you set for yourself is nearly over, or you will lose valuable effort and miss experiences that might positively inform you for decades.

Then go on the next section during the next block of time, and then the last section.

Repeat the process.

You may choose to work with another person on this activity. Compare notes—this can provide energy and certainly make

THE TEACHER I.E.P.

it interesting. Working with another may also make it easier to accomplish the tasks set, since there will be an added level of responsibility and accountability between you both.

At the end, using your notes, write a paragraph for each of the three sections addressed. Write about your experience with the exercise, about any surprises you may have encountered, and about what you learned from the effort. Was it difficult in any way? How can you use this in the future? Do you believe that it could hold value for you? How?

When you are ready, perhaps after a pause (a week? a month?), select other questions to work with in each of the three sections.

The key is to not drop the efforts when the particular exercise is over. The purpose of the exercise is to open our eyes to new possibilities, ones that might resonate with us, stay with us, and give us something to work with for a lifetime.

Continue the effort of observing yourself. It will pay off immensely, over time.

And enjoy the learning.

CHAPTER NINE

THE FUTURE

"To bear the unpleasant manifestations of others is a big thing. The last thing for a man."
—G.I. Gurdjieff

THE LONG ROLE OF THE TEACHER:

It can be argued that the role of a teacher of children and young adults would rival any other profession in both its scope and importance. From class-wide roles of instructor, disciplinarian, and motivator—to individual roles such as friend, advocate, or mentor—a teacher must continuously shift from one role to another, from one moment to the next—with overlaps constantly in the mix. To do this seamlessly is a great feat and a great gift for the students.

Yet the greatest, most far-reaching role the teacher plays is that of a molder of the future. Each of the students a teacher touches will morph, add, subtract, according to the experience they have in school. And these students are the next generation, who will then place their touch on the years ahead. Teachers influence and help create the generations

THE FUTURE

to follow after them, who will then mold their time through their own knowledge, wisdom, and character.

And still a broader vista opens up. These students not only inform their moment in time, but influence the generation to follow. As parents, they help to create the next generation of students who will enter the school system, bringing the best and worst with them. The quality of the entire loop, the cycle of *child-student-adult-parent-child* will be affected, for better or worse, by each teacher along the way in the life of a student. It is an awesome and beautiful responsibility.

One of the primary questions facing all educators is, how do we help prepare students for the future, for both their collective and individual future? Teacher preparation colleges and other such facilities help define (their view of) the needs of society into which these students will emerge. Basic needs and specific training will be addressed. Yet more and more, the importance of flexibility is being recognized. The *soft skills* such as problem-solving, communication skills, adaptability, perseverance, and the ability to adopt varied perspectives are increasingly important for the success of students as they move into their adult lives. As such, it is imperative that teachers become familiar with these soft skills themselves. We can, as teachers, foster wide-ranging skills and abilities in students to help them cope, adapt, and thrive in an uncertain future.

E.G. — AMY

Amy was in second grade and struggling to keep up with the class in reading skills. She did not have any *classification* as a special needs student, and her strong intelligence baffled adults when considering her reading. The simple fact is that as individuals we have different ways of processing information. Amy had her strengths and weaknesses.

Amy's parents brought her to my Learning Center and I ended up working intensely with her for a year. By the time she left our tutoring sessions she had progressed significantly. I expected that she would do well in school, but as it most often happens, we no longer had any contact, so I was left to conjecture or ignore.

The interesting thing here is that after fourteen years of silence I received a phone call from her father, Victor. Amy was about to graduate college with a bachelor degree. Victor was very happy and wanted to pass this on to me. "She would not have done this without your help," he said. "We are eternally grateful."

I don't relay this to toot my own horn. Teachers are constantly creating moments of learning for children. This is but one small piece of the matrix of service that a teacher can deliver in a lifetime of teaching, though of course a wonderfully valuable piece. I present this as a rare example of a teacher actually receiving long-term feedback on actions taken and support shared that may have occurred many years prior. Teachers will receive some level of immediate feedback when working with students, but not with long-term results. Regarding these results, we cannot expect to receive. We simply give.

This leads directly to the next section of this chapter:

OUR FINEST GIFT:

One of the purest and finest gifts anyone can offer is one that is given without recognition for the giver. There is in this case no giving with the hope of reward or recognition, no name on a plaque or even a quiet notice of thanks. Though there might be a reward such as a smile on a face, seeing a hungry person able to eat, or simply the feeling arising from an extension of kindness—the act of giving may be done without expectation of such recognition or even any immediate reward.

For all of the work a teacher does in the course of each day, the immediate difficulties and rewards encountered, there is constantly a giving for the future. When a student leaves a classroom, he is often not heard from or about again by the teacher. A teacher makes the efforts in the moment, in the year or so allotted for each student, and sends them off to the next stage. The results of the ripening are usually not known by the teacher. The future is being fed, not the teacher's need to know.

One deeper aspect of this giving without expectation of reward is to give from the emotions, to recognize and experience the humanity of other individuals, another area where teachers often excel. Students who connect with teachers in this way will carry the benefits for a lifetime.

EXERCISE 21:
A Clean Gift

> Do a favor for a friend or stranger. An example might be to wash some dishes that a sister has not yet gotten to do, or pick up litter in a park. Do this without any attempt at recognition for your effort. Leave no signature. Notice how differently this might feel when done for a stranger, a friend, or a nebulous "them" or "us" (as when cleaning up litter).
>
> Do this once a day for one week. Be very specific and deliberate. There is no effort here, at this time, to attempt any sort of change in personal outlook or behavior on your part or that of another. This is a specific exercise with the purpose of self-observation. What is to be seen could be illuminating, both in how one thinks and behaves. Noticing the difficulty encountered with the effort to give in this way can also be enlightening. Start with the simple (such as doing something helpful for a coworker), and move on to the less well-defined and difficult (such as practicing good-will in a moment when negative judgement begins to arise—a particularly valuable exercise) as the effort becomes stronger.
>
> It could be that the ability to plan for the future, for oneself or one's family, for all of humanity—and even for the well-being of life on a wider scale—is a uniquely human capacity. Yet,

whether it is unique or not is of little importance here (except perhaps for an associated responsibility).

This ability remains within the human capacity and distinguishes humans from those who run primarily on instinct or primal drive. It remains our choice, as well, as to whether we exercise this ability or not, and to what degree.

FREEDOM FROM ANGER:

Freedom is a small word yet a vast proposition. We can view it as a continuum—from simple (vanilla or chocolate), to complex (how do I give this child all she needs while at the same time allowing her to deeply explore her own potential, independently?). We might notice that what seems like freedom at times is really not freedom at all, such as when we take action based on habit or bias where we imagine we are exercising choice (which can be a particularly difficult moment to see), or when we allow ourselves to get swept up and "lost" in an activity. This is not freedom, no matter how good it feels, no matter how good it looks. At these times we are actually allowing ourselves to get "hooked" and pulled along. This is not to say that these experiences are bad. Not at all. They just don't represent freedom, except perhaps freedom from a bad mood or boring day.

Our target here is in the realm of deeper freedoms—freedom from the dictates of emotional, physical, and mental forces that bully us and, as we maintain our book focus, can blindly ease or spectacularly crash us into anger. We begin to see the existence of *degrees* of freedom.

Even when we isolate our study to the realm of anger and its powerful allies, we see a continuum from *gripped* to *free*. *Counting to ten* in order to hold back an angry rant represents a rudimentary form of freedom from anger. It presents freedom from the unexpected and often troubling consequences of impulsive, emotionally driven behavior, by stopping the anger from manifesting. This is an essential first step.

What we are after here, however, is a deeper freedom, where one becomes "unstuck" from the grips of anger. The goal is not necessarily to stop all anger from arising in us, or even to forever prevent the manifestation of anger. The goal is to move toward the ability to slip away from anger that comes crashing towards us, to give it no purchase. When such a position is obtained, many things change, including the option we have to act as we wish, a clean separation from emotional turmoil, and the ability to "straight-talk" another person without a hostile reaction—all quite impressive, and liberating.

Until one reaches a new level of freedom in anything, it can be difficult to see the road ahead. Some things simply are not visible until we get there. Once one attains a new level of freedom, hindsight can be most clear and exhilarating. Yet, there are still freedoms ahead, worlds of freedom that we cannot yet even imagine.

Let it be understood; there is a practical approach to moving toward freedom. Steps can be taken to increase our freedom, to free ourselves from the many limits that lurk in our environment and in our thoughts and emotions. But this is not an easy road. These new strengths must be earned. One way to fuel the efforts is to cultivate an appreciation for the process itself, as difficult as it may seem at times. "It's good. I've got this. The more challenging it is through boredom or ill-ease, the further I will grow as I not let it stop me."

STEPS TOWARD FREEDOM FROM ANGER

1. Learning how to recognize the signs of approaching anger, as well as the subtle manifestations it might display
2. Developing the ability to stop anger from bursting forth in any chosen moment, curbing explosions
3. Learning how to prevent anger from affecting us internally—to avoid anger manifesting as judgement, skewed perception, foul mood, dis-ease, etc.
4. Grappling with the parts of us that grab onto things we want and repel that which we dislike. We are, in general, very much

affected by our likes and dislikes, by what is comfortable or uncomfortable. When we don't get what we want, or get what we don't want, we fall into a "mood." Maintaining a deliberate position of *passivity with interest* will allow us to move through our moments without getting stuck to things and things not getting stuck to us. We move with ease and with clarity.

LIKES AND DISLIKES

When we automatically react to our environment, by grabbing for *this* and pushing away *that*, all day long, there is little room left for genuine interaction or response to events. All of us are programmed in our likes and dislikes to varying degrees, and our thoughts, feelings, and actions are colored by them. The irony here is that what are likely some of the most prevalent influences in our daily lives are also some of the most difficult to notice.

We live them, our like and dislikes. We identify with them. We tenaciously and automatically hold on to them, even when we think or feel we want to change. We might experience consciously or not, "Likes and dislikes are what make me who I am, and I'm sure as hell not giving *that* up."

The key word here is *automatically*. This we do without objectivity, without real choice on our part. It is as if we are not actually doing, but are being *done to*. We are *done to* by our buttons being pushed, our *pulls and pushes* being tickled. This is where anger gains purchase, where we bump into conflict; the more stuck we are in our likes and dislikes, the stronger are the bumps and conflicts—fertile ground for anger.

EXERCISE 22:
Likes and Dislikes

Select a thirty- or sixty-minute period each day where you observe with intention as many of the things, events, and moments that grab you (that you are pulled toward) and those that repel you. Observe also your reaction to the varied stimuli. In the beginning, as with many of these exercises, make no attempt at change, only observe. If change occurs, watch it, too. Note the breadth and depth of your reactive self, of the measure of time and occurrences when you are not actually in control of your feelings or actions. If it is difficult to isolate the stimuli, then notice the things that you do most often and the way you do them. You might not see the drives in you, but the manifestations of them may be far more easily seen—that is, how you think, feel, and act.

Practice this for two weeks, deciding ahead of time on five or seven days per week to practice. It's likely that anger will present itself at some point in this effort. If not, then bring forth this effort any time that anger does appear.

After this length of exercise it may become clear what the next step is for you. It could be to continue a similar effort or to expand the time window. It could be to bring intentional observation into all of the moments of one's day, as may already have begun to happen simply by making the observation efforts of this exercise.

Do not be discouraged if you find that your efforts are not producing what you want (want itself may be an example of a pull), or if it remains difficult to remember the exercise for half an hour. This is normal. If you keep gently bringing yourself back to the exercise, then it will likely get easier to maintain the effort. This is not something we are trained to do in school, at home, or in the market-place. What we are doing is going against the natural human flow of habituation. We are training ourselves to direct our attention in a specific direction. To be able to expect substantial results, this effort will need to expand, both in daily time and in overall duration—perhaps even for a lifetime.

As we make a serious effort to watch our reaction to likes and dislikes, an interesting thing begins to happen. Distance is created. We become able to observe rather than react. Our actions become less automatic. We become less reactionary, both externally and at subtle, internal levels. This then is the beginning of freedom—freedom from the grasping (at what we desire) and the pushing (at what we want to keep away).

As we practice this with emotional and mental triggers of anger, we gain freedom from this powerful force. Then we might rise above being snared, and offer something of great substance during a difficult moment or approaching disaster. Remember—it is not our likes and dislikes that binds and constricts us. It is because we ourselves are not in control, the pushes and pulls are. And when we are being controlled, our freedom shrinks. We are subject to more laws—less freedom.

Freedom from anger may manifest in different ways and at any time. Following is an example occurring outside of the classroom realm.

E.G. — GLENN: VERMONT HOLIDAY

It's Saturday, and today was to be a day of writing for this book, writing about anger—yet instead, I watch myself in a six-hour perfect buildup to the point of finding myself cursing in anger—gripped!

Here it is. I am up against it. I could easily let myself continue in this cursing mode, letting it feed and feast upon itself. My mind says no—stop this nonsense! Yet it continues to feed the anger lust—delicious abandon into rage (small rage). Today was my day to write, to reflect—a calm, relaxed day without distractions—one of two open days on this vacation weekend. It was my purpose for coming here. And all I got to do today was to deal with an emergency.

Instead of the focused day of writing in a bucolic setting, I got to wrestle with a clogged septic system in our rental property next door. I had to cut openings, dig dirt, run to town to buy tools, empty buckets of gray water from a plugged tub—and all this just to prepare for a rooter company to come in and charge an outrageous $500 to snake it all out.

I'm hungry. I'm in pain. And what I don't want to say

(because it suddenly sounds hollow) is, I deserve better than this. This is what I am really saying—and when I admit it, the righteousness begins to lose steam. Why do I deserve any specific thing simply because I expect it, or I can tally a list on one side of a ledger and expect certain results on the other (reward) side? I'm keeping quite calm so far. It just seems like the perfect setup to catch me—addressing sewage instead of quiet writing moments. It's clearly a perfect lesson for me that I can accept hour after hour, though I did feel a bit stretched. Okay, I can handle this.

But then another blow comes. To decompress a bit I decide to mow a portion of our jungle-like lawn. I try to pour gas into a lawnmower from a newly purchased gas can—and this tips the scales. The container has some ridiculous, fancy spout that is cheaply made, a worthless combination. Not only does it not do its fancy thing, but it also can't pour gasoline at all—a simple tool that can't even do its tiny job right. It's the only thing it was put on this Earth for, and it has failed miserably. Now I let loose into the anger, let it have its way with me. But a voice holds me back. No!

Now I'm angry that I can't even be angry without that damned voice of reason coming in to interfere, to belittle my feelings about the grand injustice to myself. I can't even enjoy the sweet abandon into misery and rage. So now what do I have?

At another time in my life I would have indulged this anger longer, just let it rip for a while. I might have kicked a bucket (literally only) or shouted with abandon. But at this point, after efforts upon efforts, I realize that there is actually something positive to be gained from this whole challenging day (aside from the fact that success was the final outcome of the specific sewage challenge). I was aware of the sensations of increasing anger, of building frustration, and was able to look at it from a bit of a distance. I knew that if I could keep from succumbing to the anger that I would make myself stronger. I would make my *will* stronger. I would be stronger than the anger *banging loudly at the door*. If I could keep reminding myself that this is, in actuality, a golden opportunity—another precious lesson which I could either learn from or ignore, I could gain from this. I also knew that if I didn't learn from this forced-upon-me lesson, I would see it again. It would not be finished with me—not until I am able to stand face-to-face with it and not be bested—until I could accept it simply as another experience to experience, with impartiality.

So, though I didn't get to write and relax today, I am now, at the end of the day, writing down this page of my life. I can see that I am stronger for the actions of the day, and I raise my glass and toast, "To a very fine day. May there be more (though maybe not right away)."

As I relayed this event to my brother, he suggested that the $500 spent and lessons learned were akin to taking a college course. True. And I finished the course in one day, not an entire semester. Not bad.

To summarize, observing and working with anger is like riding a wild bull (really?). If a rider in a rodeo hopped on a bull, looking to show the world and the judges his skill and ability to manage the wild beast, and the bull went tamely out to smell the flowers (as Ferdinand would) the rider would weep. There would be no prize for him, no glory, no matter what his ability. I was always impressed with the fact that the more fierce the bull, the greater the potential score for the rider, if he could stay on.

The value of studying anger lies also in its strength, its fierceness. This is what can provide each of us the possibility of "holding on" and learning much. The more powerful the anger, the more we have to gain if we are not blown away by it all. As we learn to manage or even appreciate the emotions that can so tenaciously squeeze us, the more we'll be able to deal with lesser grips that ensnare us. This all leads to a lightening of the weights which hold us back. Enlightening indeed!

It is interesting to note that numerous traditions observe freedom generally as having less, rather than more, such as with prestige or material wealth. Well-known author and Buddhist practitioner Thich Nhat Hanh speaks of freedom from a Buddhist perspective.

"Many people look for happiness outside themselves, but true happiness comes from inside of us. Our culture tells us that being happy comes from having a lot of money, a lot of power, from having a high position in society. But... many rich and famous people are not happy.

"The Buddha and monks and nuns of his time did not own anything except three robes and one bowl. But they were very happy because they had something extremely precious – freedom.

"... Here we do not mean political freedom, but freedom from the mental formations of anger, despair, jealousy, and delusion." He continues with a bit of advice. "In order to be free from anger we must practice." (1)

May the fruits of our practice lead to freedom and rich transformation!

I leave you here, reader, with a few words from John Bennett.

"The ignorant man is like a prisoner who languishes in his narrow cell, which will become his grave, because he has not learned that the door is not locked." (2)

THE PROCESS IN REVIEW

Much has been presented in this book for the reader to digest, and many jumping-off points for action may have been taken. No two individuals will approach learning in precisely the same manner. As a way of pulling the information into an overarching procedural pattern, a list outlining the process of potential effort and growth follows:

1. READ

We begin here with the written word. We have referred in the introduction and other locations to some potentials and pitfalls of a book. This window into other worlds can be a fine beginning point for a growth process to begin.

2. EXPERIENCE

Experiential study or teaching (as discussed in Chapter Five) allows a significant depth to be touched within a person. Multiple senses and overlays of receptivity give an experience considerable dimension, especially as we engage in all of these avenues of perception simultaneously.

At this stage we put our ideas, plans, and efforts into practice, as student or teacher. We take action. We create ripples and make waves.

There are many things to be seen at this stage, such as how consistent or persistent we or our students might be, how serious we are about taking our own measure, and other personal traits. We observe also the results of the particular techniques, practices, and strategies we employ—which brings us to the next stage of action in this current process.

3. OBSERVE AND ADJUST

Observation is an essential ingredient not only at this stage, but also at every stage of the processes herein discussed.

We might look for inner-driven qualities such as interest, determination, perspectives, perseverance, and will, or observe the more visible qualities of action and repetitive practices (as addressed in several chapters).

To observe and adjust (add and delete), whether in ourselves or our students, is to continually monitor and decide how to further proceed. Is our effort moving in a satisfactory direction (whether planned or not)? Shall we drop *this* portion of the effort, or tweak *that* part? Shall we continue to forge straight ahead, or drop and replace the effort entirely? This is the constant monitoring and adjusting that can help form a valuable learning experience.

4. REPEAT THE CYCLES

The goal here is to work through the cycles of *stimulus-action-observation-adjustment-action* and to do it with value. Can the cycles be turned into spirals, where a process of upward movement is created, reaching continually for loftier goals? What would this look like to you?

5. SELF AWARENESS

And still deeper will be the experience that is accompanied by an awareness of oneself while engaged in the experience. I can watch myself in action. All of the thinking, feeling, sensing experienced at deeper levels allows me to open to new perception, understanding, and insight. This essential human trait offers immense possibilities for our growth and for helping foster growth in others.

Many educational references will equate *self-awareness* with *metacognition*. While there is a close relationship between these two themes, it is worth looking into the breadth of the two. Metacognition, cognition of our cognition, is primarily a mental process (albeit a valuable process). Self-awareness, on the other hand, may include the mental as well as other aspects or our function and being (topics for another venue).

6. FREEDOM

Now we get to the deeper aim of all of our efforts, *Freedom*–freedom from anger, freedom from the limits we place on ourselves or accept from influences around us, freedom from the inner voices and habits that limit us. Freedom is a vast topic (see earlier in this chapter) affecting each of us deeply. Though the efforts might be arduous at times, the results may be worth every bit of discomfort. In the words of John Bennett, "Freedom is incomparably more precious than the good opinion of others or our own self-esteem." (3) What is freedom worth to you? What are you willing to invest?

7. SHAPE THE LEARNING

At this point we do not stop at the particular levels of freedom we attain. Beyond personal freedom is the freedom we can bring to others. The effort here is to package the learning, the experience, so as to then be able to verbalize the process and communicate this to those around us. The learning and freedom become available to carry into other spheres.

8. PASS IT ON

As we pass on our learning experiences we enable the *learning-cycles* to become *spirals* of learning and growth. As the expanding process of learning and sharing becomes familiar to those we touch, it then can affect an even greater number.

A teacher will always be teaching, even in the still or chaotic moments when direct teaching is not in play. We will always be sharing something. We will always be role models. We affect the students, who become parents, who bring forth new students and teachers, and on.

Thus, the spiral grows.

END-OF-CHAPTER QUESTIONS

1. What is the average amount of time you get to work with a student? How much growth can you observe in that time?
2. Have you experienced giving without receiving? Was it intentional or not? Describe the experience.
3. What would be your definition of freedom?
4. Describe freedoms that have been granted you as you matured. Have you wanted more? Do you still want more?
5. Do you have experience of freedoms that you have intentionally sought and attained, or are in process?
6. Which portions of this book have spoken most loudly to you?
7. Which material from this book can you most directly use to enhance your classroom or relationship with children/students?

APPENDIX

ENDNOTES

CHAPTER TWO

1. *Oxford English Dictionary Online*, s.v. "perspective," https://en.oxforddictionaries.com
2. *Merriam-Webster Online*, s.v. "perspective," https://www.merriam-webster.com/dictionary
3. Lindsay Lennon '07, "Study Abroad: A World of Opportunity," *NEW PALTZ: The Alumni Magazine of the State University of New York at New Paltz* 33 (Spring 2015): 8.
4. Ibid.
5. Julie A. Gorlewski and David A. Gorlewski, *Making it Real: Case Stories for Secondary Teachers* (Rotterdam, Netherlands: Sense Publishers, 2012), 5.
6. Daniel P. Hallahan, James M. Kauffman, and Paige C. Pullen, *Cases for Reflection and Analysis for Exceptional Learners: An Introduction to Special Education, 11th ed.*(Boston: Pearson, 2009), 109.
7. Ibid., 99.
8. Gorlewski and Gorlewski, *Making it Real*, 1.
9. P.D. Ouspensky, *In Search of the Miraculous* (New York: Harcourt, Brace & World, 1949), 126.

CHAPTER THREE

1. Dan Kindlon and Michael Thompson with Teresa Barker, *Raising Cain: Protecting the Emotional Life of Boys* (New York: Ballantine Books/Random House, 1999), 9.
2. William Golding, *Lord of the Flies* (New York: Perigree/Putnam Publishing Group, 1954), 64.
3. Lois Lowry, *The Giver* (Boston: Houghton Mifflin Company, 1993).
4. *Oxford English Dictionary Online*, s.v. "anecdotal notes," https://en.oxforddictionaries.com
5. *Dictionary.com*, s.v. "anecdotal notes," https://www.dictionary.com
6. Kerry Gallagher, Terry Magid, and Kobie Pruitt, "The Educator's Guide to Student Privacy," ConnectSafely.org (May 20, 2016): https://www.connectsafely.org/eduprivacy/
7. Institute of Education Sciences/National Center for Education Statistics (March 1997): https://nces.ed.gov/pubs97/web/97859.asp

CHAPTER FOUR

1. A. L. Stavely, *Where is Bernardino?* (Aurora, Oregon: Two Rivers Press, 1982), 18.
2. Dr. Carey J. Green, "Success Skills for School and Career," podcast audio on the importance of communication skills, *The Best of Our Knowledge*, WAMC, January 12, 2018.
3. Laura S. Kastner and Jennifer Wyatt, *Getting to Calm: Cool-headed Strategies for Parenting Teens + Tweens* (Seattle: ParentMap, 2009).
4. Jeanna Bryner, "Most Students Bored at School," Live Science.com (February 28, 2007): https://www.livescience.com/1308-students-bored-school.html
5. "The Music and Movements of Gurdjieff," The DuVersity.org: https://www.duversity.org/music/music.html

CHAPTER FIVE

1. Staveley, *Where is Bernardino?*, 28.
2. Maryellen Weimer, "Benefits of Giving Students Choices," *The Teaching Professor* (blog), November 29, 2017, https://www.facultyfocus.com/articles/teaching-professor-blog/benefits-giving-students-choice-learn/
3. Stavely, *Where is Bernardino?*, 15.
4. David Kolb, *Experiential Learning* (Englewood Cliffs: Prentice Hall, 1984), 38.
5. Amanda Wiesner-Groff, "Creating a Stimulating Classroom Environment: Definition & Strategies," Study.com, chapter 11/lesson 6, https://study.com/academy/lesson/creating-a-stimulating-classroom-environment-definition-strategies.html
6. "The Effects of a Stimulating Learning Environment: A pilot project with Ohalo Academic College, Quatzrin (Israel) and Steelcase Education," Steelcase Corporation/Steelcase.com, https://www.steelcase.com/research/articles/topics/classroom-design/effects-stimulating-learning-environment/

CHAPTER SIX

1. Hallahan, Kauffman, and Pullen, *Exceptional Learners*, 12.
2. Ibid., 8.
3. DSM-5: Diagnostic and Statistical Manual of Mental Disorders, Fifth Edition, (2013 text revision).
4. Valerie Paradiz, *Elijah's Cup* (London & Philadelphia: Jessica Kingsley Publishers, 2005).
5. Hallahan, Kauffman, and Pullen, *Exceptional Learners*, 266.
6. Laura Archera Huxley, *You Are Not the Target: A Practical Manual of How to Cope with a World of Bewildering Change* (Los Angles: Wilshire Book Company, 1974).
7. Kindlon and Thompson, *Raising Cain*
8. Oleta Garrett Fitzgerald, "Pipeline to Prison: Special education

too often leads to jail for thousands of American children," *The Hechinger Report*, hechingerreport.org, https://hechingerreport.org/pipeline-prison-special-education-often-leads-jail-thousands-american-children/
9. Hallahan, Kauffman, and Pullen, *Exceptional Learners*, 285.
10. R. A. Barkley, "Behavioral Inhibition, Sustained Attention, and Executive Functions: Constructing a Unifying Theory of ADHD," *Psychological Bulletin* 121: 65-94.
11. Ibid.

CHAPTER SEVEN

1. *Oxford English Dictionary Online*, s.v. "mindfulness," https://en.oxforddictionaries.com
2. Dana Santas, "Beyond 'Namaste': The benefits of yoga in schools," *Special to CNN*, updated 7:55 a.m. ET, May 10, 2016, https://www.cnn.com/2016/05/10/health/yoga-in-schools/index.html
3. *Oxford English Dictionary Online*, s.v. "metacognition," https://en.oxforddictionaries.com
4. *Dictionary.com*, s.v. "metacognition," https://www.dictionary.com
5. Rae Jacobson, "Metacognition: How Thinking about Thinking Can Help Kids—A powerful skill for building resilience," Childmind.org, https://childmind.org/article/how-metacognition-can-help-kids/
6. Tamara Rosier, in "Metacognition: How Thinking about Thinking Can Help Kids—A powerful skill for building resilience," Childmind.org, https://childmind.org/article how-metacognition-can-help-kids/
7. *Oxford English Dictionary Online*, s.v. "empathy," https://en.oxforddictionaries.com
8. *Dictionary.com*, s.v. "empathy," https://www.dictionary.com
9. Gwen Dewar, "The case for teaching empathy: Why empathy doesn't 'just happen,'" Parenting Science.com, https://www.parentingscience.com/teaching-empathy.html
10. Ibid.

11. Brianna Crowley and Barry Saide, "Building Empathy in Classrooms and Schools," *Education Week*, January 20, 2016, edweek.org, https://www.edweek.org/tm/articles/2016/01/20/building-empathy-in-classrooms-and-schools.html
12. Terry Heick, "Education vs. True Connection" in *Teaching Empathy: Are We Teaching Content or Students?*, Edutopia (blog), February 10, 2015, https://www.edutopia.org/blog/teaching-empathy-content-or-students-terry-heick
13. Colin Ryan, "Saved by the Belle" (episode 1609) in *Moth Grand Slams: Life and Death on The Moth Radio Hour*, WAMC, aired Friday 6/2/18, https://themoth.org/story-library/stories/
14. Yoga In Schools (YIS), Pittsburgh, Pennsylvania, https://yogainschools.org
15. Santas, https://www.cnn.com/2016/05/10/health/yoga-in-schools/index.html
16. Alan Reder, "Dealing with Anger through Understanding and Control," *Yoga Journal* (August 28, 2007), https://www.yogajournal.com/yoga-101/unmasking-anger
17. "Benefits of Yoga in Schools," *Yoga4Classrooms* (2018), http://www.yoga4classrooms.com/benefits-of-yoga-in-schools
18. J. G. Bennett, *Transformation* (Sherborne, England: Coombe Springs Press, 1978), v.

CHAPTER EIGHT

1. Hallahan, Kauffman, and Pullen, *Exceptional Learners*

CHAPTER NINE

1. Thich Nhat Hanh, *Anger* (New York: Riverhead Books/Penguin-Random House), 1-2.
2. Bennett, *Transformation*, 28.
3. Bennett, *Transformation*, 193.

www.ingramcontent.com/pod-product-compliance
Lightning Source LLC
Chambersburg PA
CBHW032224080426
42735CB00008B/702